GUINNESS WORLD RECORDS Amazing Animals

by Vicky Shiotsu and Shirley Pearson

Carson-Dellosa Publishing LLC
Greensboro, North Carolina

Credits

Content Editor: Christine Schwab
Copy Editor: Julie B. Killian
Layout and Cover Design: Van Harris

Carson-Dellosa Publishing LLC
PO Box 35665
Greensboro, NC 27425 USA
www.carsondellosa.com

ISBN 978-1-60996-461-0
01-335111151

TABLE OF CONTENTS

SETTING GUINNESS WORLD RECORDS RECORDS

Guinness World Records accomplishments are facts or events that belong in one of eight categories:

- Human Body
- Amazing Feats
- Natural World
- Science and Technology
- Arts and Media
- Modern Technology
- Travel and Transport
- Sports and Games

Some records are new because they are exciting and involve events that have never been attempted before. People with unique talents or features are also permitted to become record setters. However, many of the records are already established, and people try to find records that they can break. One record holder, Ashrita Furman, has broken or set more than 300 records since 1979.

Guinness World Records receives more than 60,000 requests each year. Record setters and breakers must apply first so that their attempts are official. The organization sets guidelines for each event to make sure that it can be properly measured. Guinness World Records also makes sure that all record breakers follow the same steps so that each participant gets an equal chance. Professional judges make sure that the guidelines are followed correctly and measured accurately. However, the guidelines may designate other community members who can serve as judges to witness an event. Once the record attempt is approved, the participant gets a framed certificate. The person's name may also be included in the yearly publication or on the Guinness World Records Web site at *www.guinnessworldrecords.com*.

BE A RECORD BREAKER!

Hey, kids!

Tubby is a Labrador retriever that collected and recycled about 26,000 plastic bottles from his daily walks. Rob Williams (USA) made a sandwich with his feet in less than two minutes. Tiana Walton (UK) placed 27 gloves on one hand at one time. Aaron Fotheringham (USA) landed the first wheelchair backflip. The Heaviest Pumpkin ever weighed 1,725 pounds (782.45 kg). And, Rosi, the Heaviest Spider ever, is larger than a dinner plate. What do all of these stories have in common? They are Guinness World Records records!

A world record is an amazing achievement that is a fact. It can be a skill someone has, such as being able to blow the largest bubble gum bubble. It can be an interesting fact from nature, such as which bird is the smelliest bird. Guinness World Records has judges who set rules to make sure that all record setters and record breakers follow the same steps. Then, the adjudicators (judges) count, weigh, measure, or compare to make sure that the achievement is the greatest in the world.

So, can you be a Guinness World Records record breaker? If you can run, hop, toss, or even race with an egg on a spoon, you just might see your name on a Guinness World Records Certificate someday. With the help of an adult, visit *www.guinnessworldrecords.com*. There you will find a world of exciting records to explore—and maybe break!

 The Carson-Dellosa Team

Tubby the "Green" Labrador

Most Bottles Recycled by a Dog
2010

Tubby is a dog with a nose for recycling. In the past six years, Tubby has collected about 26,000 plastic bottles on his daily walks. Tubby is a Labrador retriever. His owner, Sandra Gilmore (UK), walks him twice a day. On each walk, Tubby usually finds at least three plastic bottles that have been thrown away. Tubby crushes them in his teeth, removes the lids, and brings them to his owner. She recycles them. Gilmore says that Tubby has always loved fetching plastic bottles, even as a puppy. He likes bottles more than balls and sticks. Is it because of the wonderful crackling noise that plastic makes when squished? Gilmore thinks so.

● Plastic lasts for years. That's why it is so important to recycle. Below is a list of things that can be made from recycled plastic. Recycling symbols cover some of the letters. Replace each recycling symbol with a letter and write the letters on the lines. (Hint: The number inside the triangle represents the missing letter, where A is 1 and G is 7.)

[3][1]rp[5]ts ___ ___ ___ ___ ___ ___ ___

[3]loth[5]s ___ ___ ___ ___ ___ ___ ___

[5][7][7] [3][1]rtons ___ ___ ___ ___ ___ ___ ___ ___ ___

[6]urnitur[5] ___ ___ ___ ___ ___ ___ ___ ___ ___

L[1]wn [3]h[1]irs ___ ___ ___ ___ ___ ___ ___ ___ ___ ___

Pip[5]s ___ ___ ___ ___ ___

Til[5] ___ ___ ___ ___

Tr[1][6][6]i[3]li[7]hts ___ ___ ___ ___ ___ ___ ___ ___ ___ ___ ___ ___ ___

Baby Boom

Most Dolphins Born in a Year in a Single Facility
December 4, 2008

In 2008, the Xcaret (pronounced Ish-ca-ret) Park in Mexico welcomed 11 brand-new calves. That's right. Dolphin babies are called calves. But, these calves didn't moo—they whistled. They didn't run—they swam. And, their births made it possible for the park's Delphinus Xcaret dolphinarium to be awarded the Guinness World Records record for the Most Dolphins Born in a Year in a Single Facility.

The dolphinarium at Xcaret has a wonderful bottlenose dolphin breeding program. The average survival rate for calves born in captivity is 60 percent. It is even lower in the wild. In 2008, all 11 of those new bottlenose dolphin calves survived. That's an amazing survival rate of 100 percent.

● Below are 11 dolphins. Each tells a dolphin fact. One letter is missing from each sentence. Write the missing letters, in order, to spell the name of the largest dolphin in the world. The answer may surprise you!

1. Sharks attac___ dolphins.

2. Adult males are b___gger than females.

3. Dolphins have a___l of their teeth by the time they are five months old.

4. Only one ca___f is born at a time.

5. Calves stay with their moth___rs for six years.

6. A dolphin b___eathes through a blowhole.

7. A newborn bottlenose dolphin ___eighs about 45 pounds (20 kg).

8. Dolphins' eyes are on the sides of their ___eads.

9. Dolphins are mamm___ls.

10. Some females babysit other dolphins' ca___ves.

11. Dolphins hav___ fantastic hearing.

___ ___ ___ ___ ___ ___   ___ ___ ___ ___ ___
1   2   3   4   5   6   7   8   9   10 11

CD-104534

Roll Away!

Fastest Caterpillar

If caterpillars had a race, one would be the clear winner. That would be the larva of the mother-of-pearl moth. It is the world's Fastest Caterpillar. It can travel 15 inches (38.1 cm) per second. That's a rate of almost 1 mile per hour (1.6 km/h)! But, it doesn't always move at this speed. It only goes this fast when it feels threatened. If danger is near, the caterpillar curls up into a ball. Then, it rolls away! The caterpillar's speed helps it survive.

● The world's Fastest Caterpillar has a body made up of several segments, or parts. Find out how many by reading the clues. For each clue, find the matching number on a leaf and cross it out. Then, complete the sentence at the bottom of the page with the number that is left.

- It is not 20 + 20.
- It is not 50 – 40.

- It is not 13 + 10.
- It is not 48 – 40.

- It is not 56 – 20.
- It is not 32 – 12.

- It is not 11 + 11.
- It is not 23 – 20.

- It is not 10 + 15.
- It is not 27 – 10.

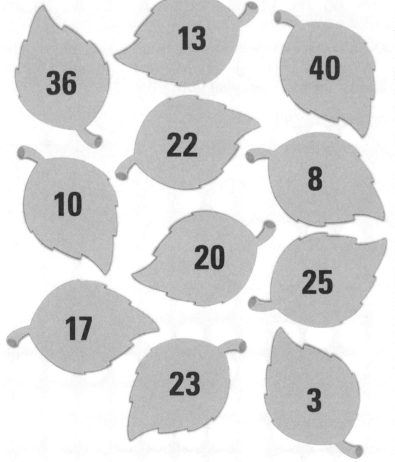

The body of the world's Fastest Caterpillar is made up of _____ segments.

A Freezing Life

Most Cold-Resistant Amphibian

The wood frog is a little frog that is only 1 to 3 inches (2.5 to 7.6 cm) long. It lives anywhere from the U.S. state of Georgia to the Arctic Circle. Until recently, few scientists bothered to study this amphibian. But, that has all changed.

The wood frog is the Most Cold-Resistant Amphibian in the world. In the Arctic winter, the frog's body freezes solid. But, it doesn't die. Its blood is packed full of sugar. The sugar protects the frog's brain and other vital organs. When spring arrives, its heart restarts and pumps blood back into its body. Within 24 hours, the frog is croaking and leaping, happy to be alive. Why does this excite scientists? If the frog's heart still works after being frozen, maybe the human heart can too! Doctors hope to save lives by using this science to freeze human hearts for organ transplants.

● The wood frog's Latin name is *Rana sylvatica*. How can you change RANA into LIFE for transplant patients? Change one letter at a time! Starting with the word RANA, change exactly one letter to make a new word. Write the new word on the lines below RANA. Continue changing one letter of your newest word at a time until RANA has transformed into LIFE. Use the clues to help. (Hint: The boxes indicate the letters to change.)

R   A   N   A

___ ___ ___ [ ]   A bell might have done this yesterday.

___ [ ] ___ ___   A bell might do this today.

[ ] ___ ___ ___   The sound a bell makes.

___ ___ ___ [ ]   What you do at dinner.

[ ] ___ ___ ___   You probably write on one of these in a notebook.

L   I   [ ]   E

CD-104534

What's That Smell?

Smelliest Bird

Some birds may be dull to look at. Some may be dreadful to hear. Some may be unpleasant to touch. But, no bird could possibly smell as bad as cow manure, could it? Think again. The hoatzin of Colombia holds the undesirable record of being the Smelliest Bird in the world. This South American bird has beautiful head plumage that makes it delightful to look at, but only from a distance. A diet of leaves and a cow-like digestive system combine to create a suffocating stink. The word *hoatzin* is pronounced "what-seen" but "what-smell" might make more sense!

● Smell is not a sense you usually think of when a bird flies by. Below are seven action phrases. Every action involves one or more of your five senses (sight, smell, sound, taste, touch). Which of your senses would you use the most in these actions (primary senses)? Which other senses would you use? What sense do you think would not be involved in this action? Write your answers on the lines.

Action Phrases	Primary Sense(s)	Secondary Sense(s)	Sense(s) Not Involved
ask a question	_____	_____	_____
hold a snake	_____	_____	_____
scratch a rash	_____	_____	_____
nibble a cookie	_____	_____	_____
open an oven	_____	_____	_____
throw a ball	_____	_____	_____
zip a zipper	_____	_____	_____

CD-104534

Can You Hear Me?

Noisiest Land Animal

How loud can you yell? Chances are you won't be louder than the male howler monkey. This animal found in Central and South America holds the record for the Noisiest Land Animal. The male howler monkey makes a loud wailing noise that can be heard 3 miles (4.82 km) away! He uses his big voice to warn other monkeys to stay away. This way, he is able to keep them from invading his home.

● **Solve the problems. Write the answers on the lines to learn more facts about howler monkeys.**

1. 23 + 7 − 10 − 5

　　Both male and female monkeys weigh about _____ pounds.

2. 14 + 9 − 13 + 10

　　Howler monkeys live in groups called troops. A troop usually has up to _____ members.

3. 16 + 5 − 13 + 7

　　Howler monkeys spend about _____ hours a day sleeping.

4. 25 − 5 + 11 − 1

　　Howler monkeys' tails are about _____ inches long. They use their tails for grabbing things and for hanging from branches.

A "Beary" Big Appetite

Hungriest Bear Species

Have you heard the phrase "hungry as a bear"? Whoever invented it may have been thinking about the giant panda. The animal spends up to 15 hours a day eating! No wonder this type of bear has been named the world's Hungriest Bear Species!

The giant panda feeds on bamboo. It eats 20 to 40 pounds (9 to 18 kg) of food every day! Bamboo doesn't have a lot of nutrients. That's why the giant panda needs to eat a lot of it. The nutrients help the bear grow and stay healthy. The giant panda weighs 200 to 250 pounds (90 to 113 kg). It eats more food for an animal its size than any other kind of bear.

● Help the giant panda search for bamboo. Start at the center. Then, go along the path, collecting five numbers as you go. The line from the fifth number must lead back to the center. (Do not go over any part of the path more than once.) Color the path that gives you the greatest sum.

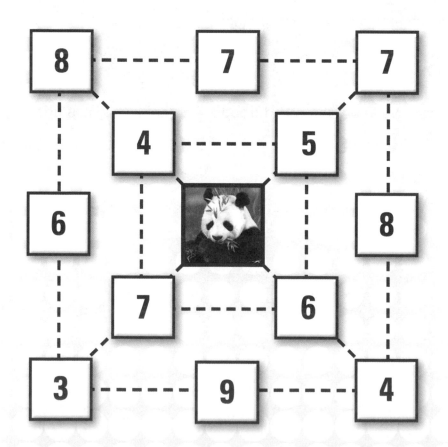

CD-104534

Don't Call Me Honey!

Most Fearless Mammal

The Most Fearless Mammal in the world is not a lordly lion, a terrible tiger, or even a gruesome grizzly. It's a medium-sized mammal that lives in Africa and Asia. When full grown, this mammal weighs only 15.4 to 28.7 pounds (7 to 13 kg). Its favorite food is honey, but don't let that fool you. The honey badger is anything but sweet. Its skin is so tough that bee stings, porcupine quills, and snakebites rarely bother it. A honey badger will challenge any creature that wanders too close to its burrow. It has been known to attack buffalo, hunters, and even cars.

● The word *badger* has another meaning. It can be used as an action word or verb. It means "to bother or annoy over and over again." Other animal names can also be used as verbs. Below are eight sentences. Each is missing a word that is both a verb and an animal name. Using the word bank, write the missing words.

Word Bank			
bug	duck	fly	slug
chicken	fish	monkey	wolf

1. Did you see that baseball batter _____ the ball?

2. Do you prefer to _____ in the lake or the ocean?

3. Does your little sister _____ you too?

4. Don't _____ down your dinner so fast.

5. I would like to learn how to _____ an airplane.

6. Is the runner going to _____ out of the race?

7. That clown sure likes to _____ around.

8. Dylan had to _____ his head to avoid the tree branch.

A Jumping Superstar

Most Jump Rope Jumps by a Dog in One Minute
August 8, 2007

One, two, three, four, five! On and on jumped Sweet Pea on August 8, 2007. This energetic dog jumped her way to a Guinness World Records record on live TV. She made 75 jumps in 1 minute and set a world record! In fact, she broke her own record by 10 jumps!

Sweet Pea trains with her owner, Alex Rothacker (USA). The two work hard every day. Jumping is just one of the many tricks that Sweet Pea can do. For example, Sweet Pea can climb up a flight of stairs. What's so amazing about that? She does this while balancing a glass of water on her nose!

● **Read about another dog and owner. Then, solve the problem.**

Erin has heard about Sweet Pea. Now, she wants to train her dog, Spike, to do tricks too. To get started, Erin goes to the store and buys a jump rope and a ball. She pays $1.75 for the two items. The jump rope costs 75¢ more than the ball. How much does each item cost?

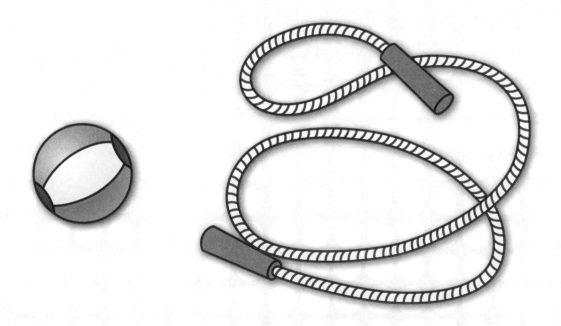

The jump rope costs $_____, and the ball costs $_____.

CD-104534

Amazing Albert

Fish with the Largest Repertoire of Tricks
October 25, 2005

Dean Pomerleau (USA) is a teacher. Instead of learning reading and writing, Pomerleau's students learn tricks. Instead of receiving report cards, his students receive food. And, instead of learning by sitting still in a classroom, his students swim freely around a tank full of water. That's because these students are pet fish. His prize pupil, Albert, was a calico fantail goldfish. Albert holds the record for the Fish with the Largest Repertoire of Tricks.

● Albert was one smart goldfish. He was named for a brilliant scientist. Listed below are some of the tricks that Albert learned to perform. Write the missing letters, in order, to spell this goldfish's brainy last name.

Swim through a long T U N N ____ L.

Do the L ____ M B O.

Feed from his O W ____ E R ' S hand.

Kick a ____ O C C E R ball into a net with his snout.

Fetch a ball from the B O ____ T O M of the tank.

Dunk a B A S K ____ T B A L L through a hoop.

Kick a football between the U P R ____ G H T S.

DA ____ C E to music.

This goldfish's brainy last name is

____ ____ ____ ____ ____ ____ ____ ____ .

Standing Tall

Tallest Mammal

Most people know that a giraffe is tall. In fact, it is the Tallest Mammal in the world. An adult male stands 15 to 18 feet (4.6 to 5.5 m) tall. That's taller than the height of most classrooms!

The tallest known giraffe was a male named George. He was born in Kenya, Africa. George was 19 feet (5.8 m) tall. In 1959, he was brought to a zoo in England. He was so tall that his horns almost touched the roof of the zoo's Giraffe House!

● You have learned that male giraffes grow to be 15 to 18 feet tall. Try these math challenges with the numbers 15 and 18.

Write the numbers 3 to 8 in the circles so that the three numbers along each side add up to 15. Two numbers have been provided for you.

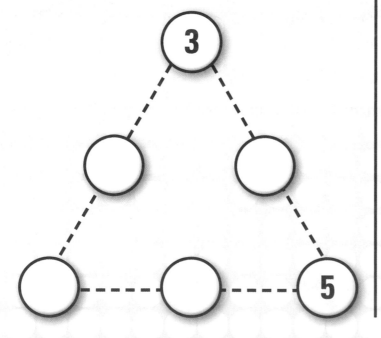

Write the numbers 4 to 9 in the circles so that the three numbers along each side add up to 18. Three numbers have been provided for you.

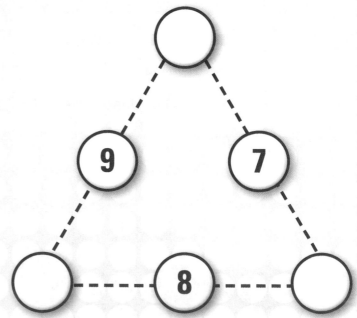

CD-104534

Nice Nose!

Keenest Sense of Smell in a Bird

Just because a bird has a hard beak doesn't mean it can't smell. The black-footed albatross holds the record for the Keenest Sense of Smell in a Bird. It can sniff out food up to 18 miles (29 km) away! This enormous bird is completely dependent on the sea. A female only comes ashore to lay her eggs. The black-footed albatross nests mostly in the northern Hawaiian Islands. Pairs of these birds mate for life, producing only one chick each year. The black-footed albatross may travel more than 9,300 miles (15,000 km) from her nest in search of food for her baby. The bird's fantastic sense of smell helps it locate fish in the sea. The albatross has extra-large nostrils and is one of a group of birds called "tubenoses."

● Below are partial names of some foods that the black-footed albatross locates by scent. Write the missing vowels to reveal the seabird's smelly diet.

C R ___ S T ___ C ___ ___ N S	Use the boxed vowels, in order, to complete this sentence:	H ___ R R ___ N G
F ___ S H [ ] ___ L		K R ___ L L
F ___ S H ___ G G S	Sailors consider seeing an albatross to be a sign of	P L ___ N K T [ ] N
F L Y ___ N G F ___ S H	G ___ ___ D L ___ C K.	S Q [ ] ___ D

Open Wide

Largest Mouth of a Terrestrial Mammal

Has your dentist ever looked into your mouth and asked you to "open wide"? If you were a hippopotamus, you would have no problem! That's because the hippo has the largest mouth of any land animal. When an adult male hippo says, "Aah," his mouth can stretch 4 feet (1.2 m) wide!

If you could peek into a hippo's mouth, you would see some very big teeth. Some are as long as a person's arm! The largest teeth can grow up to 2.5 feet (46 cm) long. The teeth may not look that long to you though. That's because only part of each tooth sticks up above the gum line.

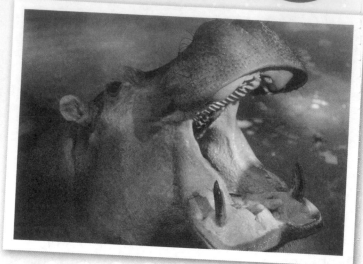

● **Some hippos are standing by a river. Read the clues to solve the problems.**

Thirty-six hippos are standing in a line.

The first hippo has its mouth open.

The next two hippos have their mouths closed.

The next three hippos have their mouths open.

The next four hippos have their mouths closed.

1. If the pattern continues, is the mouth of the 30th hippo open or closed?

   _____

2. How many hippos have their mouths open? _____

   How many hippos have their mouths closed? _____

What a Sweetie

Oldest Kinkajou Ever in a Zoo
2003

Sugar Bear, a kinkajou, was one of the Honolulu Zoo's sweetest animals. In 2003, he was more than 40 years old, and he holds the record for the being the Oldest Kinkajou Ever in a Zoo. Because kinkajous are only active at night and spend all of their time in trees, scientists don't know much about them. They can only guess that a wild kinkajou probably doesn't live as long as Sugar Bear did!

Kinkajous are related to raccoons and red pandas. They have huge round eyes and long fluffy tails. Because they are nocturnal, they need those big eyes to see in the dark. They use their tails to grasp branches and wrap around tree trunks while climbing. Those fluffy tails also keep them warm at night. Kinkajous live in the Americas as far north as southern Mexico.

Sugar Bear needed a lot of quiet time in his old age. He spent most of his time in his den and was often heard snoring. Sugar Bear's keeper petted and scratched him and made sure he was well fed.

● Kinkajous love fruit. So did Sugar Bear. Follow the instructions to discover the name of Sugar Bear's favorite fruit.

1. The first letter in the second word of SUGAR BEAR   ——

2. The first two letters in the word ANIMAL   —— ——

3. The middle letter in the word KINKAJOUS   ——

4. The second consonant in the word HONOLULU   ——

5. The vowel that appears twice in the name RED PANDA   ——

That's Spooky!

Fish with the Most Eyes

Many strange-looking fish live deep in the oceans. One of these is the spookfish. This animal lives 300 to 3,000 feet (91 to 910 m) below the surface of the Pacific Ocean. As its name suggests, the fish looks spooky! This odd-looking creature has four main eyes and another pair of "eyes" that act like mirrors. It holds the record for the Fish with the Most Eyes.

The spookfish lives where there is little light. It uses one main pair of eyes to see. The others help the fish focus and take in light, helping the fish see better in the dark waters.

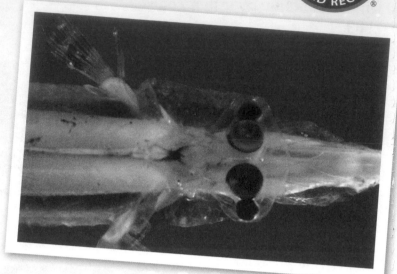

● Here is another strange-looking fish. It is made up of many squares. How many squares can you count in all? _____

CD-104534

What Am I?

Most Unclassifiable Mammal

What critters snack on ants and termites, have pig-like snouts, dig with incredibly strong claws, and have tubes for teeth? African aardvarks! Their peg-like teeth are their strangest part. Scientists call the African aardvark *Tubulidentata* ("tube teeth"). No other living mammal can match that smile! Although aardvarks have no close relatives, don't feel too sorry for them. The aardvark leads the way in front of every other animal in one important place—the dictionary!

● Other animals have strange teeth too. Using the clues and the spaces provided, match the teeth with the correct animal.

1. I am a rodent just a little bigger than a mouse. I have four long teeth outside, not inside, my mouth, so I don't eat dirt while I am digging. I can even wiggle my teeth one tooth at a time.
   WHAT AM I? ___ ___ ___ ___ ___   ___ ___ ___ ___ ___ ___

2. I am a fish that lives on the sea bottom. Don't let my small size fool you! There's a reason I am named for my scary teeth. My enormous mouth and dagger-like teeth are perfect tools for hunting.
   WHAT AM I? ___ ___ ___ ___ ___ ___ ___ ___ ___

3. I am a big reptile like my cousin the alligator. When I hatch, a fake tooth on top of my snout helps me crack through my eggshell. This "egg tooth" is really part of my leathery skin.
   WHAT AM I? ___ ___ ___ ___ ___ ___ ___ ___ ___

4. I am a mammal that lives in the sea. I have two enormous upper teeth made of ivory that can grow to 4.5 feet (1.5 m) in length. Sometimes, I use them to help me "walk."
   WHAT AM I? ___ ___ ___ ___ ___ ___

5. Some people call me a monster of the sea, probably because of my two rows of 3-inch-long (7.6 cm) triangular teeth. I can lose thousands of teeth in my lifetime, but I just grow more.
   WHAT AM I? ___ ___ ___ ___ ___   ___ ___ ___ ___ ___
   ___ ___ ___ ___ ___

6. I don't have any top teeth, but I don't need them. I spend all day chewing grass and hay with other grazers.
   WHAT AM I? ___ ___ ___ ___ ___

crocodile

fangtooth

naked mole rat

sheep

great white shark

walrus

Doggie Kisses

Longest Tongue on a Dog
August 5, 2009

Have you ever been licked by a dog? That's probably a sign that the dog likes you. Puggy the Pekingese is great at showing his Texan owner how much he cares. Licking is something this little dog does very well. That's because Puggy holds the record for the Longest Tongue on a Dog. His tongue is 4.5 inches (11.43 cm) long from snout to tip. Puggy's tongue is about half as long as he is tall. That makes for a lot of doggie kisses!

Pekingese are small, usually between 6 and 9 inches (15.2 and 22.9 cm) tall. They weigh less than 14 pounds (6.4 kg). They have long, straight hair and flat faces. In ancient China, they were called "lion dogs." Chinese emperors kept the smallest of these dogs in the sleeves of their coats. Today, mini Pekes are still called "sleeves."

● Puggy has licked up some alphabet soup, creating seven words that have something to do with Puggy and Pekingese dogs. The last letter of the first word is the same as the first letter of the next word, and so on. Circle each word that Puggy has eaten. The first word has been circled for you.

PEKINGESEMPERORECORDOGSLEEVESTRAIGHTONGUE

CD-104534

A "Leggy" Pet

Largest Millipede
August 1, 2003

Jim Klinger (USA) has a strange pet. It is an African giant black millipede. A millipede is an animal that looks like a worm. It has many legs. Most millipedes like Klinger's grow to be up to 11 inches (28 cm) long. But, Klinger's pet is just over 15 inches (38 cm) long! It is also more than 2.5 inches (6.5 cm) around! No wonder it has been named the world's Largest Millipede. It is so long that if you set its body straight on this sheet of paper, the millipede would not fit.

● How many legs does the Largest Millipede have? To find out, compare each number on the millipede with the clues. Cross out the numbers that do not fit the four clues. When you are done, use the number that is left to complete the sentence at the bottom of the page.

Clues

1. The ones digit is greater than the tens digit.

2. The tens digit is greater than the hundreds digit.

3. The sum of the digits is greater than 12.

4. The number is even.

Klinger's millipede has _____ legs.

Sharp Eyes

Keenest Vision by a Bird

The peregrine falcon is a hunting bird. It lives on every continent except Antarctica. This bird can spot a target from very far away. In fact, the peregrine falcon holds the record for the Keenest Vision by a Bird. It can see three or more times better than a person can. Believe it or not, this sharp-eyed bird can spot a pigeon that is 5 miles (8 km) away!

The peregrine falcon is a fast flyer too. It can travel faster than any other animal. When this bird hunts, it soars through the air. If it sees food below, it will start to dive. It can reach speeds of up to 200 miles per hour (320 km/h) as it dives toward its food!

● You have just learned that the peregrine falcon has excellent eyesight. Now, test yours! Look at the set of triangles. The letters stand for the points of the triangles.

A

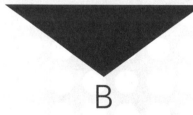

B

Is B closer to A or closer to C?

_____

Check your answer by measuring the distance from A to B and from B to C.

What did you find out?

_____

_____

_____

C

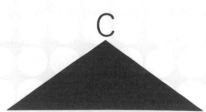

CD-104534

Mistaken Identity

Slowest Fish

The Slowest Fish in the sea has a snout like a straw that it uses to suck up plankton. It has a tail like a monkey that it uses to grab coral and seaweed. The male has a pouch like a kangaroo that it uses to hold its babies. And, it has a head like a horse. What is it called? A sea horse!

Sea horses range from 0.25 inches (0.6 cm) to 1 foot (30 cm) in length. They have fins on their heads that they use for steering and spinal dorsal fins to help them swim. Unlike their four-legged namesakes, these horses are slow. They actually move faster without bothering to swim. They float along with the current.

● A sea horse is a fish; a horse is not. Other sea creatures share their names with animals that don't live in the sea. Below is a list of sea creatures. Some names are real, and others are not. For each name, decide if it is real or fake. Circle the corresponding answer letter. The circled letters, from left to right, will spell the name of a sea horse relative.

Sea Creature Name	sea cow	sea hare	sea jackal	sea lion	sea llama	sea mouse	sea partridge	sea spider	sea squirrel
Real?	S	E	F	D	L	A	M	O	I
Fake?	B	J	A	K	R	H	G	C	N

Jump, Frog, Jump!

Farthest Jump by a Frog
May 21, 1977

Frogs are great jumpers. Many can leap up to 20 times their body length. That's like a person jumping more than 100 feet (30.5 m)! A frog named Santjie set the record for the Farthest Jump by a Frog. This little green jumper was a South African sharp-nosed frog. Its long legs were made for leaping!

Santjie took part in a jumping contest called a frog derby. The contest was held in Petersburg, South Africa. The frog leaped a total of 33 feet 10 inches (10.3 m). The length was found by adding the lengths of three leaps in a row. Santjie's amazing jump was equal to about half the length of a basketball court!

● **Read the story about another little frog. Then, solve the problem.**

A frog is jumping along the ground when it falls into a pit. The pit is 50 feet deep. The frog decides that jumping out is no problem. On his first jump, he leaps 10 feet in the air and then slides back 5 feet. On his second jump, he leaps another 10 feet and then slides back 5 feet again. If the frog continues with this pattern, how many jumps will it take for him to get out of the pit? (Hint: Draw a picture of the pit. Mark how far up the frog jumps each time.)

It would take _____ jumps.

Jumping Guinea Pigs

Longest Jump by a Guinea Pig
July 27, 2009

A guinea pig named Diesel made record-breaking news in 2009. That was the day he made the Longest Jump by a Guinea Pig. The stunt took place in London, England. The event marked the release of a new movie. In the movie, guinea pigs are trained as spies.

Ten guinea pigs in all tried the long jump. Diesel won by clearing a gap of about 8 inches (20.5 cm)! The people who saw the stunt were impressed. A guinea pig is only about 10 to 14 inches (25 to 36 cm) long. That means Diesel jumped almost the length of his body! It proved that even a guinea pig could be an athlete!

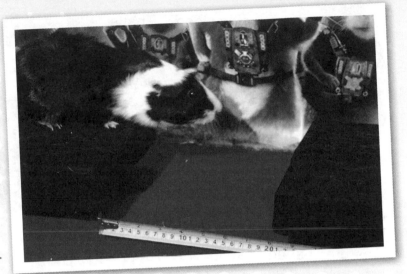

● Imagine that some guinea pigs are getting ready to do the long jump. Before they jump, use the three numbers on their blocks to complete the pairs of math problems. For each problem, use each of the numbers once.

1.

2 4 5

$$\begin{array}{r} 6\ 3\ \square \\ +\ \ \square\ 7 \\ \hline 6\ 8\ \square \end{array} \qquad \begin{array}{r} \square\ 3\ 7 \\ -\ \ 1\ \square \\ \hline 5\ \square\ 3 \end{array}$$

2.

1 6 9

$$\begin{array}{r} 2\ \square\ 3 \\ +\ \square\ 8\ \square \\ \hline 4\ 5\ 2 \end{array} \qquad \begin{array}{r} 7\ \square\ \square \\ -\ 2\ 4\ 3 \\ \hline 4\ 7\ \square \end{array}$$

3.

3 7 8

$$\begin{array}{r} \square\ 0\ 4 \\ +\ 2\ 2\ \square \\ \hline 9\ \square\ 2 \end{array} \qquad \begin{array}{r} 9\ 5\ 1 \\ -\ 5\ \square\ \square \\ \hline \square\ 6\ 4 \end{array}$$

CD-104534

Nap Time

Sleepiest Mammal
November 2006

"Did you have a nice sleep?" That's probably what Dr. Fritz Geiser said to the tiny Australian eastern pygmy possum after it woke up from sleeping for 367 days in the lab. That's more than a year of dreaming! Dr. Geiser is a zoologist. He studies hibernation.

The pygmy possum lives in southeastern Australia and Tasmania. Although the weather there isn't usually very cold, the pygmy possum is still able to hibernate. Before going to sleep, these mouse-like creatures eat and eat and eat. Then, they drift off to sleep. While hibernating, these possums use very little energy. They take this energy from fat stored in their bodies.

● Imagine that a sleeping pygmy possum is dreaming of food. Because she is so sleepy, the dream words are all mixed up. Using the word bank, unscramble the possum's food dreams.

Word Bank

fruit	insects	nuts	scorpions	spiders
honey	nectar	pollen	seeds	worms

---

1. ceinsst
_____

2. cinooprss
_____

3. ehnoy
_____

4. ellnop
_____

5. deess
_____

6. acenrt
_____

7. firtu
_____

8. morsw
_____

9. deiprss
_____

10. nstu
_____

CD-104534

Top Dog

Tallest Dog Living
February 15, 2010

In the world of dogs, one Great Dane is a towering giant. That's Giant George. He stands 43 inches (1 m) from the top of his shoulders to the bottom of his paws. He holds the record for the Tallest Dog Living. Giant George also weighs an amazing 245 pounds (111 kg). That's more than the weight of most men!

David and Christine Nasser (both USA) take care of Giant George. The three live in Tucson, Arizona. When Giant George stands beside the Nassers, he looks more like a small horse than a dog! His large body requires a huge amount of food. To keep in tip-top shape, Giant George eats 110 pounds (49.9 kg) of food each month. That's about twice as much as a collie eats!

● Figure out how to make a model showing how tall Giant George is. Imagine that you have some large toy blocks. Some are 5 inches high, while others are 7 inches high. You are going to stack the blocks one on top of the other. How many will you need of each type of block to make a tower that is exactly the same height as Giant George? (The dog is 43 inches tall.)

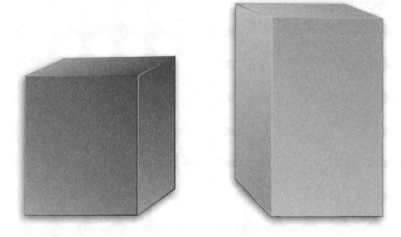

You will need _____ 5-inch blocks and _____ 7-inch blocks.

CD-104534

What's in a Name?

Mammal with the Most Names
December 12, 2002

A cat is a just a cat, right? Not when that wild cat is a puma. The *Puma concolor* ("cat of one color") of the Americas holds the record for the Mammal with the Most Names. This wild cat is known by more than 40 different names in English alone. Add names from languages spoken in South and Central America, and the puma will answer to anything!

● The picture below is divided into 31 labeled pieces. These labels are names of wild cats found in North, Central, and South America. About half of the names refer to the puma; about half do not. Color the pieces that you think name this special wild cat. If colored correctly, a picture of the "American Lion" will be revealed.

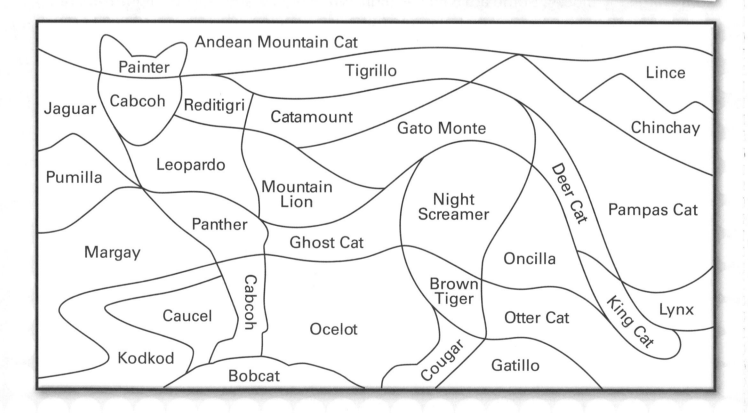

A Swimming Champ

Fastest Swimming Bird

Penguins are great swimmers. Although they waddle on land, they "fly" gracefully under the water. One type of penguin holds the record for being the Fastest Swimming Bird in the world. That record holder is the gentoo penguin. It can reach bursts of speed of almost 17 miles per hour (27 km/h)!

The gentoo penguin is easy to spot. For one thing, it has a bright orange-red bill. It also has a white patch around each eye. This speedy swimmer is a good diver too. It can dive more than 328 feet (100 m) deep in the water!

● Many penguins live in Antarctica where it is cold and icy. Imagine that some gentoo penguins are standing around the blocks of ice below. The penguins are getting ready to dive into the water.

Look at the picture carefully. How many blocks of ice can you count in all? _____

Poisonous Package

Smallest Species of Rattlesnake

If you are walking in the woods in the southeastern United States, be careful where you step. The pygmy rattlesnake holds the record for the Smallest Species of Rattlesnake in the world. Adults are smaller than 18 inches (45 cm) in length. Curled up, their dull coloring and blotchy spots make them look like harmless round pinecones. Baby pygmy rattlesnakes are even smaller. They look exactly like their parents except for the ends of their tails, which have no rattles and are yellow. When curled, they would just barely cover the top of a quarter.

Most rattlesnakes will warn you with a loud rattle. But the pygmy rattlesnake won't! Its rattle sounds more like the buzzing of an insect than the rattle of a poisonous viper. And, that's if the pygmy rattlesnake bothers to rattle at all. Most of the time, the tail rattles are broken and silent. Scientists believe that the pygmy's thin, wriggly tail end has become more useful as bait for possible prey than as a warning signal to possible predators.

● Below is a pygmy rattlesnake marked with spots that contain letters. Cross out any letters that are found in the word INSECTS, which pygmy rattlesnakes eat when they can't find any lizards or frogs. Write the remaining letters, in order, to spell what Texans call this wriggly, poisonous package.

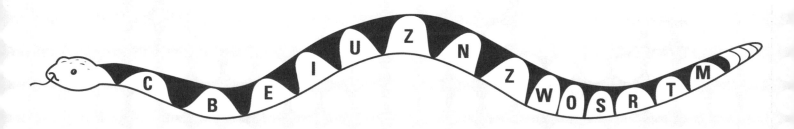

___ ___ ___ ___ ___ ___ ___ ___

All in the Family

Longest Rabbit
April 6, 2010

Darius is a Flemish giant rabbit. In 2010, he measured 4 feet 3 inches (129 cm) long. He set the record for the world's Longest Rabbit.

Darius comes from a family of record setters. His mother held the record for Longest Rabbit just before he did. Alice was 3 feet 3 inches (99 cm) long. Alice's mother, Amy, held the record before that. She was 2 feet 8 inches (81 cm) long. All three rabbits were raised by Annette Edwards (UK). It seems she has a knack for raising healthy, "hoppy" rabbit families!

● **Here is another family of rabbits: Cotton, Fluffy, Thumper, and Wiggles. Read the clues about them. Then, write their names in order from the shortest rabbit to the longest.**

• Fluffy is longer than Thumper.

• Cotton is longer than Wiggles.

• Thumper is shorter than Cotton.

• Cotton is not the longest rabbit.

• Wiggles is not the shortest rabbit.

The rabbits in order from shortest to longest:

_____, _____, _____, _____

Do You See What I See?

Greatest Color Vision

People can see about 10,000 colors. We see seven primary colors in a rainbow. All of these colors come from red, green, and blue. Stomatopod crustaceans have even better eyes than people. These shelled creatures can't see rainbows because they live in the ocean. But, if they could, they would see more colors than just seven. Stomatopods can see at least eight primary colors.

The mantis shrimp is a stomatopod. It is able to see food that other animals might not notice at all. These crustaceans use colors on their bodies for signaling other stomatopods. Parts of their bodies are colored differently depending on whether they want to mate or fight. Stomatopods are small animals that are usually only 8-10 inches (30 cm) long. But, they are very aggressive and have huge claws. They use their heavy club claws to crack open their prey and their sword-shaped claws to spear their prey.

● Below are four mini crossword puzzles. Each puzzle contains two color words that share a common boxed letter. Using the word bank, complete the puzzles. Then, write the letters in the numbered boxes in order on the lines below to spell another name for the vicious mantis shrimp.

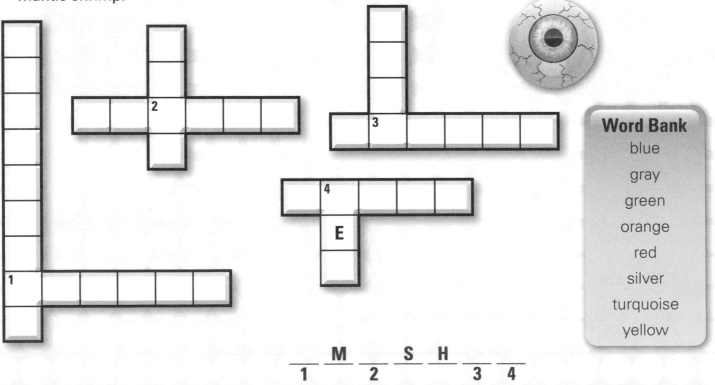

Word Bank
blue
gray
green
orange
red
silver
turquoise
yellow

$\underline{} \ \underline{M} \ \underline{} \ \underline{S} \ \underline{H} \ \underline{} \ \underline{}$
1   2   3   4

Highest Jump by a Pig
August 22, 2004

It is no surprise to learn that ponies can run, pelicans can fly, and penguins can swim. How about a potbellied pig that can jump? Now, that's a surprise. Kotetsu is a potbellied pig that lives on a farm in Japan. In 2004, Kotetsu completed a jump that shocked pig owners around the world. His record leap measured 27.5 inches (70 cm) in the air. Most potbellied pigs grow no taller than 18 inches (45.7 cm) from hoof to shoulder. With that amazing jump, Kotetsu could have easily leaped over another pig!

Potbellied pigs can make great pets. They are gentle and easy to train. They love to play and, with care, can live well into their teens. These pigs don't have great eyesight, but their hearing and sense of smell are excellent. One drawback to having potbellied pigs as pets is their weight. They are pigs, after all, and even miniature pigs such as potbellies can weigh 150 pounds (67 kg). At that size, it is tough to cuddle a full-grown potbellied pig in your lap.

● Below are some adjectives that describe pets. Each adjective starts with the same letter and sound as the pet it describes. Some pets, such as the potbellied pig, may be more unusual than others. Write the names of pets that the adjectives may describe. (There may be many correct answers.)

Bossy   **bird** _____

Cheery _____

Curious _____

Fast _____

Gentle _____

Goofy _____

Hungry _____

Lazy _____

Messy _____

Rascally _____

Slithery _____

Trusting _____

Dragon Tales

Largest Lizard

Did you know that a certain kind of dragon is alive and well? It is the Komodo dragon, and it is really a lizard. The Komodo dragon is the Largest Lizard in the world. It lives on the islands of Indonesia in Southeast Asia. A male grows to be about 7 feet 5 inches (2.25 m) long. It can weigh about 130 pounds (59 kg).

The largest known Komodo dragon was a male. He was given to an American scientist in 1928. The lizard was 10 feet 2 inches (3.1 m) long and weighed 365 pounds (166 kg)! Now, that was a dragon worth bragging about!

● **Learn more facts about the Komodo dragon. Use the clues to find the mystery numbers. Then, write the numbers on the lines to complete the sentences.**

1. A Komodo dragon has sharp teeth. How many teeth does it have?

   Clues: You say the number when you count by 3s, 4s, and 5s.

   The number is between 40 and 80.

   A Komodo dragon has _____ teeth.

2. A Komodo dragon eats a lot! The bigger it is, the more food it needs. How many pounds of food can a 120-pound Komodo dragon eat in one meal?

   Clues: You say the number when you count by 2s, 3s, and 8s.

   The number is between 75 and 100.

   A 120-pound Komodo dragon can eat _____ pounds of food in one meal.

 CD-104534

A Skateboarding Pro

Fastest 100 Meters on a Skateboard by a Dog
July 30, 2009

Tillman the English bulldog loves to skateboard! He gets restless if he can't ride his skateboard every day. In July 2009, he showed off his skills in Los Angeles, California. The dog covered 100 meters in 19.6 seconds. That set a record for the Fastest 100 Meters on a Skateboard by a Dog!

How is it that Tillman can skateboard so well? His owner, Ron Davis (USA), thinks part of the answer lies in the dog's warm-up method. He says that Tillman always chews on the wheels of his skateboard before going out to ride!

● Imagine that a dog named Romper will try skateboarding. Read the clues and use the calendar to find out when his skateboarding lesson will be.

1. Romper and his owner will go out of town on the first Saturday of the month. They will be gone for 5 days.

2. Romper spends all day at a dog park on the 2nd and 4th Sundays of each month. He can't skateboard on those days.

3. Romper visits his pal Ruff on Thursdays and Fridays. He can't skateboard then.

4. The skateboarding lesson will not be during the week of the 20th.

5. The skateboarding lesson will not be on a school day.

6. The lesson will be on an even-numbered day.

Sunday	Monday	Tuesday	Wednesday	Thursday	Friday	Saturday
			1	2	3	4
5	6	7	8	9	10	11
12	13	14	15	16	17	18
19	20	21	22	23	24	25
26	27	28	29	30		

When is Romper's skateboarding lesson?
It is on the _____ day of the month.

CD-104534

Highest-Ranking Camel
April 5, 2003

Bert is a Los Angeles reserve deputy sheriff in California (USA). He helpfully teaches children about the dangers of drug use. He outstandingly represents his department at fairs and festivals. He proudly wears a badge. But, never ever will you catch Bert in a police uniform. At about 1,800 pounds (816 kg), none will fit. Bert prefers it that way.

Bert is a one-humped camel, or dromedary. He is the Highest-Ranking Camel in the world. Bert has been with the San Dimas Sheriff's Department since 2003. He has never caught any criminals, but he does a lot of good.

● Deputy Bert has a duty to his department, which he performs well. People who work in police departments have many different duties and job titles, including deputy. Some of these titles are listed below. A second list contains words that can be found scrambled within those job titles, just as the word *duty* can be found within the word *deputy*. Match the job titles with the correct words.

1. captain ____ 　　　　　　　　　　　　　　**A.** crane

2. commander ____ 　　　　　　　　　　　　**B.** deep

3. commissioner ____ 　　　　　　　　　　**C.** dive

4. detective ____ 　　　　　　　　　　　　**D.** duty

5. inspector ____ 　　　　　　　　　　　　**E.** greet

6. investigator ____ 　　　　　　　　　　**F.** invite

7. lieutenant ____ 　　　　　　　　　　　　**G.** mission

8. sergeant ____ 　　　　　　　　　　　　**H.** pant

9. superintendent ____ 　　　　　　　　**I.** price

10. deputy ____ 　　　　　　　　　　　　**J.** tilt

Bug Power

Strongest Animals

If you held a contest for the world's Strongest Animals, what animals do you think would win? Believe it or not, the answer is beetles! Ounce for ounce, the larger beetles of the tropics are the world's Strongest Animals.

Think of how small the beetles' bodies are. Then, think about the loads they carry. Some of these insects can lift up to 850 times their own weight! That would be like a person carrying 850 friends! Beetles are even stronger than elephants. That's because elephants can carry only one-fourth of their weight.

● Beetles don't exercise and lift weights to get stronger, but people do. Below are some weights that a person might practice lifting. Write the numbers 6 to 14 on the lines so that three numbers in each row, column, and diagonal add up to 30. Three of the numbers have been provided for you.

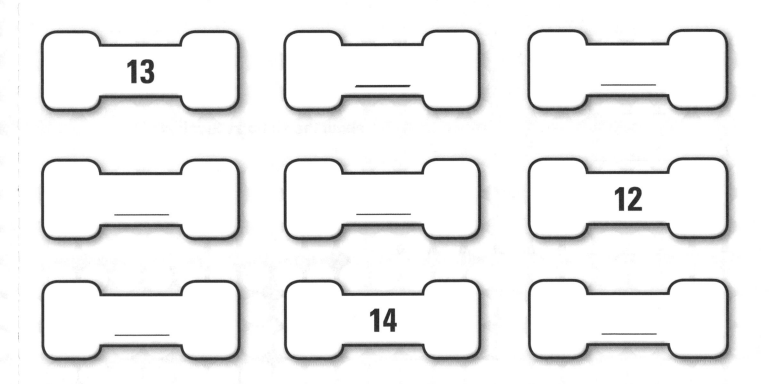

Swallow, the Cow

Smallest Cow (Height)
September 14, 2009

The Smallest Cow (by Height) in the world is a Dexter cow named Swallow who lives in the United Kingdom. Dexters are naturally smaller than most cows, but Swallow is the smallest of all. A cow's height is measured from hind foot to hip. Swallow reaches only 33.5 inches (85 cm). That's not even as tall as five stairs!

● Think of some other animals and compare their sizes. Match each letter in Swallow's name with the first letter of a new animal name. Write this new name beside the matching Swallow letter. Is this animal smaller than Swallow, about the same as Swallow, or much taller than Swallow? Write that animal's name on a line that you think matches its height. Think about your answers. An animal such as bear may have surprising results. A polar bear is much taller than Swallow, but a koala bear is much smaller. *Bear* is a general answer; *polar bear* is specific.

much taller than Swallow

_____

S _____   _____

W _____   _____

about the same as Swallow

A _____   _____

L _____   _____

L _____   **smaller than Swallow**   _____

O _____   _____

W _____   _____

          _____

Fast-Food Star

Fastest-Eating Mammal
February 2005

● To discover the name of the world's Fastest-Eating Mammal, write the missing letters in the paragraphs below. Then, write the letters in order on the lines.

Elephant ☆ aren't the only creatures

wi ☆ h unusual noses. Another much

sm ☆ ller mammal with a more

st ☆ angely shaped ☆ ose exists. Few pe ☆ ple have seen this peculiar animal. It

lives mo ☆ tly underground in swampy areas of east ☆ rn North America. It has a naked

pink nose that is shape ☆ like a star. Its nose is fringed with 22 tiny tentacles. More than

100,000 nerve fibers connect the animal's nose to its brain. This makes its nose five times more

sensitive to touch than the human hand.

This animal is the Fastest-Eating Mam ☆ al in the world. Its nose plays a huge part in its

feeding, whether digging in the ground ☆ r swimming in water. Within only 120 milliseconds

(about one-eighth of a second), this tiny animal can sense, catch, and eat its prey. In comparison,

it takes people more than five times that long to even begin stopping at a red traffic ☆ ight.

With this world r ☆ cord fast-food title, this animal is truly a star.

_____ _____ - _____ _____ _____

CD-104534

A Fishy Problem

Largest Teeth Compared to Head Size for a Fish
January 1, 2002

The Sloan's viperfish lives deep in the ocean. This strange-looking fish holds the record for the Largest Teeth Compared to Head Size for a Fish. Its slender body is about 11 inches (28 cm) long. Its head measures 0.8 inches (2 cm) long. But, its fang-like teeth measure 0.5 inches (1.3 cm). Each tooth is more than half the length of the fish's head!

The viperfish's teeth are too large to fit inside its mouth. Instead, they curve over the jaws when the mouth is closed. To eat, the fish must open its mouth wide to make the jaws vertical. That's the only way its prey can pass into its throat!

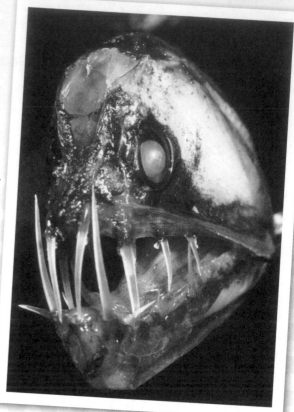

● Here is another interesting fish. It is made of 1 bead and 8 toothpicks. How would you move the bead and 3 toothpicks so that the fish is facing the other way? Draw a picture of how the fish would look.

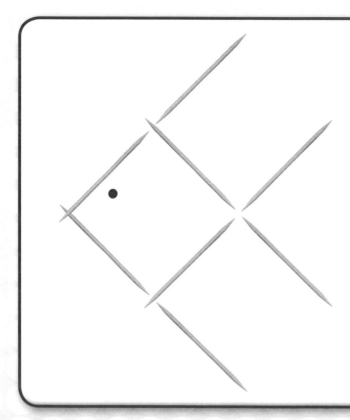

Elephant Artists

Most Expensive Painting by Elephants
February 19, 2005

Imagine that you and seven friends get together to paint a picture. You paint for six hours, taking 15- to 20-minute hourly breaks for rest and a snack of sugarcane and hay. Your finished masterpiece measures 7 feet 10 inches (2.39 m) tall and 26 feet 3 inches (8 m) long. It sells for $39,000!

In 2005, that's exactly what Kamsan and her friends did. Their painting is titled *Cold Wind, Swirling Mist, Charming Lanna I.* Unlike you, Kamsan and her friends didn't use their hands. They used their long, gray trunks! Kamsan is an elephant. She and about 70 other elephants live at the Maesa Elephant Camp in Thailand. The camp trains Asian elephants and their drivers to work and perform in a natural environment. The animals perform whatever skills they are able to learn.

● Below are the eight artistic elephants, including Kamsan. They are labeled by their names and the names of skills taught at the camp. The names of the skills are missing letters. Write the missing letters in order, and they will spell a phrase that Thai poets use for the word *elephant*.

 KONGKAM
____ive pe____ple rides

 AU POD
play the harm____ ____ica

 LANKAM
gather sti____ks

 DUANPEN
____aul logs

 PUNPETCH
give mass____ges

 SONGPUN
pl___y darts

 KAMSAN
play ____ith a soccer ball

 WANPEN
da____ce

___ ___ ___ ___ ___ ___ ___ ___ ___

Up in the Treetops

Largest Tree-Dwelling Mammal, 2004

What red-haired animal species lives in the trees of Asia's tropical rain forests? The answer is the orangutan. This long-haired ape is the Largest Tree-Dwelling Mammal in the world. The male weighs about 183 pounds (83 kg) and is about 5 feet (1.5 m) tall. The female weighs about 110 pounds (50 kg) and stands about 4 feet (1.2 m) tall.

Orangutans are known for their long, reddish hair, but their arms are long too! When orangutans stand upright, their hands reach their ankles! Their lengthy arms help them swing through the trees with ease.

- Write the missing numbers and add your way to the top of the rain forest trees. The two numbers next to each other must add up to the number above them.

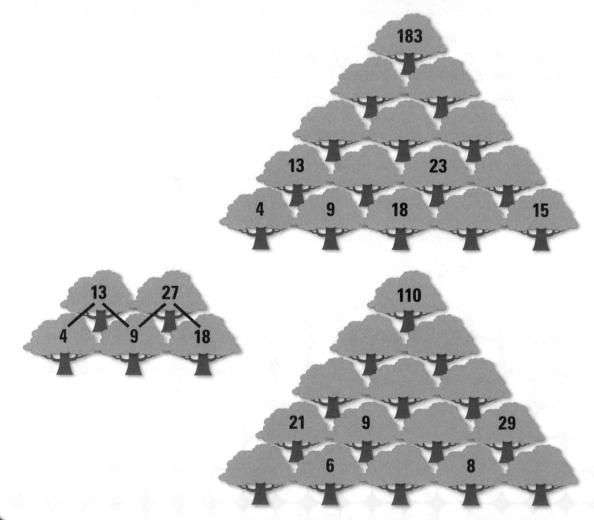

183

13   23

4   9   18   15

13   27

4   9   18

110

21   9   29

6   8

All Tied Up

Most Knots Undone by a Dog in Three Minutes
September 26, 2010

Claudia Neumann's (Germany) little black dog, Ben, is an expert at untying knots. In 2010, Ben performed in front of an audience of about 4,000 people. Several fans volunteered to have their hands tied behind their backs. Ben managed to undo 14 of those knots in three minutes using just his teeth.

Ben is a shih tzu hybrid. He is very well trained. Neumann, a veterinary nurse, has taught him more than 100 commands. Ben is also a movie star and is always happy to perform for the camera. He performs in commercials, TV, and films. Ben is very smart. He will free you if you are tied up, but be careful! He is likely to take money right out of your wallet before he lets you go. That's one of his movie tricks!

● Below are 10 other tricks that Ben has mastered. The first list shows the commands; the second list completes them. Using the letters, match each command to the rest of the trick.

1. drink _____

2. fetch _____

3. jump _____

4. play _____

5. pretend _____

6. ride _____

7. drive _____

8. roll _____

9. unroll _____

10. walk _____

A. a ball

B. a car

C. a mat

D. from a straw

E. on top of a donkey

F. out of a shopping cart

G. over

H. soccer

I. to be dead

J. upright on back legs

An Egg-stra Large Egg

Largest Egg from a Living Bird
May 17, 2008

Gunnar and Kerstin Sahlin (both Sweden) are used to seeing large eggs. That's because they own an ostrich farm. Ostriches lay the largest eggs of any living animal. An average ostrich egg weighs about 3.3 pounds (1.5 kg). That's about the size of 24 chicken eggs!

In 2008, the Sahlins got a big surprise. One of their ostriches had laid an extra-large egg. The Sahlins rushed to the post office to have it weighed. The egg weighed a whopping 5 pounds 11 ounces (2.6 kg)! It set a record for the Largest Egg from a Living Bird!

● Read the story about some ostrich eggs. Then, solve the problem.
(Hint: Each child in the story has fewer than 10 eggs.)

Jay and Keisha lived on an ostrich farm. Each child held a basket of ostrich eggs.

Jay said to Keisha, "If you give me one of your eggs, I'll have double the number you have."

Keisha replied, "If you give me one of your eggs, then our baskets will be equal."

How many eggs does each child have?

Jay has _____ eggs, and Keisha has _____ eggs.

Giant Rodent

Largest Rodent

The capybara is the world's Largest Rodent. A rodent is an animal with front teeth it uses for gnawing. This grass-chewing animal grows to be about 4 feet (122 cm) long and stands about 2 feet (61 cm) tall. It can weigh up to 174 pounds (79 kg)! Some people think the capybara looks like a giant guinea pig!

Capybaras live in Central and South America. They make their homes in the swamplands. These rodents love the water. They can stay underwater for up to five minutes. Sometimes, they will even sleep underwater with their noses poking out for air!

● Use the grid to find out what the word *capybara* means. Each symbol below shows a letter's position in the grid. Write the letters that match the symbols. (Example: ⊏ stands for the letter O.)

A	E	F
G	R	O
M	S	T

The word capybara means

___ ___ ___ ___ ___   ___ ___ ___ ___ ___

Blazing Swordfish

Hottest Fish Eyes

Swordfish regularly dive deep into ocean water as chilly as 41°F (5°C). They must be able to see their moving prey in the murky darkness, or else they will starve. Swordfish don't carry flashlights. But, they have something even better—large eyes, which are almost four times bigger than ours, and brain "heaters." These heaters can warm their brains to as much as 57°F (14°C) above water temperature. With eyes able to heat up to 82°F (28°C), seeing and catching dinner becomes easy. Similarly sized fish without these special heaters might take up to 12 times longer to catch identical meals. Having the Hottest Fish Eyes means getting fresh dinner!

● In the sentence below, replace the underlined words with appropriate rhyming words to discover how the swordfish's heating system compares with the heating systems of other large fish. The starting letters of each correct rhyme are contained in the air bubbles below.

Tuna and **come sparks** have similar **seating** systems **chat beat** some or all of their bodies, **hut** swordfish **rust** concentrate on **weeping** their eyes and **plains dot** and ready for **punting**.

S H BR H B M H SH K TH H

Tuna and ____ ____ ____ ____ ____ ____ ____ ____ ____ ____ have similar ____ ____ ____ ____ ____ ____ ____ systems ____ ____ ____ ____ ____ ____ some or all of their bodies, ____ ____ ____ swordfish ____ ____ ____ concentrate on ____ ____ ____ ____ ____ ____ their eyes and ____ ____ ____ ____ ____ ____ ____ ____ ____ and ready for ____ ____ ____ ____ ____ ____ .

Longest Insect
October 16, 2008

The world's Longest Insect looks more like a stick than a bug! Chan's megastick is a type of insect called a walking stick. It lives in the rain forests of Borneo, an island in Southeast Asia. Chan's megastick measures 22.3 inches (56.6 cm) long with its legs stretched flat. It is about as long as an adult person's arm!

Chan's megastick is long, but it hides well in the trees. That's because it looks like a twig. Maybe that's why this insect has only just been discovered. Only three of these mega-insects have ever been seen.

● Find out how much of Chan's megastick's length is made up of its body. Color the spaces with prime numbers red. (A prime number is divisible by only 1 and itself.) Color the other spaces yellow. When you are done, a number will appear. Use it to complete the sentence at the bottom of the page.

4	3	10	2	9	17	12
		18	23	25	11	15
21	19	24	27	31	7	29	13
6	37	33	45	26	35	41	38
39	43	49	51	57		47	55

The body of Chan's megastick is _____ inches long.

No Rush for This Critter

Slowest Mammal

You can probably walk a mile (1.6 km) in 20 minutes. But, for the Slowest Mammal in the world, that walk would take more than half a day—that is, if it could even walk. But, it can't! Instead, the three-toed sloth uses strong claws (three on each foot) to pull itself along the ground at a speed of 6 to 8 feet (1.8 to 2.4 m) per minute. The sloth moves faster in the treetops of the South American rain forests, but even then, it only travels up to 15 feet (4.6 m) per minute.

Sloths are so slow that algae grow on their grayish-brown hair, causing them to look green! That's not a bad thing for the sloths. Hanging very still, upside down, and covered in camouflage makes it hard to be spotted by predators such as jaguars.

● All animals move in different ways, depending on the shapes of their bodies, where they live, what they eat, and what is hunting them. On the left is a list of animals. Match each of these animals to its movement by writing the letter label on the line beside the animal. For some creatures, there may be more than one answer.

1. cow _____		**A.** climb
2. fox _____		**B.** crawl
3. frog _____		**C.** dig
4. hamster _____		**D.** hop
5. kangaroo _____		**E.** jump
6. lizard _____		**F.** leap
7. monkey _____		**G.** run
8. rabbit _____		**H.** soar
9. seagull _____		**I.** swim
10. swordfish _____		**J.** trot
11. worm _____		**K.** walk
12. zebra _____		**L.** wiggle

Soaring Cindy

Highest Jump by a Dog
October 7, 2006

Cinderella May a Holly Grey is a special name for a special dog. Cindy is a greyhound. In 2006, she competed in a special Dog Challenge in Missouri. Cindy jumped over a pole that stood 68 inches (172.7 cm) off the ground! That feat earned her the record for the Highest Jump by a Dog. Cindy is amazing in other ways too. The greyhound is a therapy dog. She visits schools and sits with children as they read storybooks.

● Some dogs were practicing high jumps. Read the clues. Then, use the grid to help you match the dogs with their colors and jump heights.

Clues:

• Chip did not jump the highest.

• The white dog made the lowest jump.

• Tupper jumped higher than Lacy.

• Lacy is not a brown dog.

• The black dog jumped the highest.

	Height in Inches			Color		
	18	27	36	brown	black	white
Tupper						
Chip			X			
Lacy						
brown						
black						
white						

Tupper   color: _____   jump height: _____ inches

Chip   color: _____   jump height: _____ inches

Lacy   color: _____   jump height: _____ inches

CD-104534

The Case of the Growing Goldfish

Longest Goldfish
March 24, 2003

Joris Gijsbers (Netherlands) has a pet goldfish. Does he keep it in a tiny fishbowl by the side of his bed? Probably not. Gijsbers's pet is the world's Longest Goldfish, measuring 18.7 inches (47.4 cm) long! That's about 10 times the length of a regular goldfish. Some people believe that the larger the goldfish bowl, the larger the goldfish will grow.

● Goldfish are common pets that come in many different varieties including bubble eye, comet, and shubunkin. Below are two rows of fishbowls. In each row, each bowl is slightly bigger than the previous one. The scrambled words inside the bowls grow progressively longer too. One by one, unscramble the words in the bowls and write them on the lines underneath. Put together the two starred words to find out the name of another type of goldfish.

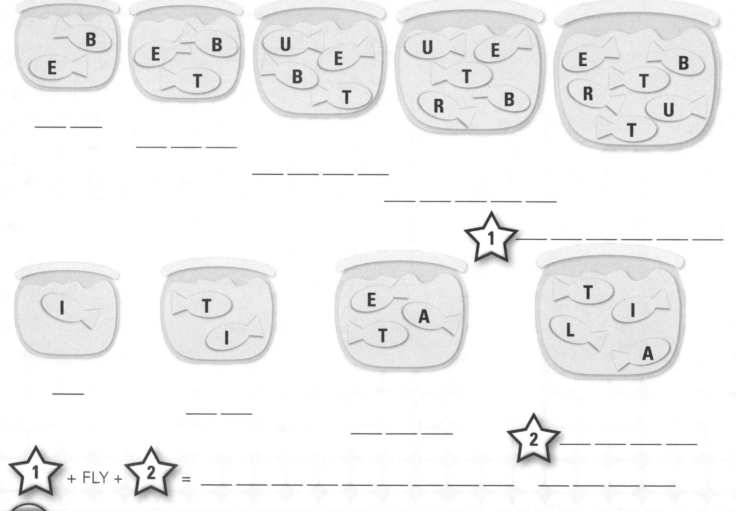

1 + FLY + 2 = _____ _____

Beautiful Rosi

Heaviest Spider
July 27, 2007

Rosi has long legs and beautiful black hair. She is also a world record holder and is famous. Rosi lives in Austria with her owner, Walter Baumgartner. Her family is originally from the rain forests of South America. Rosi is a spider but not just any spider. Rosi is a kind of tarantula called the Goliath bird-eating spider. She is the Heaviest Spider in the world.

In 2007, Rosi weighed exactly 6.17 ounces (175 g). Her leg span is more than 10 inches (25.4 cm), and she is too big to fit on a dinner plate! Tarantulas are hairy spiders. They have sharp teeth called fangs, and their bites may be poisonous. But, even if Rosi were to bite you, the bite would just feel like a bee sting. Tarantulas are scary looking, but they are not harmful to people. They are night hunters that catch their prey with their fangs. They eat lizards, frogs, and birds but mostly feast on insects. Their poisonous venom helps them digest their food. Female tarantulas can live up to 25 years in captivity. Rosi may be with her owner for a long time.

● A tarantula has 2 main body parts, 8 eyes, 2 fangs, 2 pairs of spinnerets, 4 pairs of legs, and 7 segments in each leg. For each body part, use the associated number to find a word in the text that occurs exactly that number of times and fits exactly in the space provided.

How Many	Body Part	Word from Text
2	main ⌐b¬ody parts	b ___ ___ ___
8	eye⌐s¬	___ s
2	fa⌐n¬gs	___ ___ ner
2	pairs of s⌐p¬innerets	p ___ ___ ___ ___ ___ ___
4	p⌐a¬irs of legs	a ___ ___
7	⌐s¬egments in each leg	___ ___ s ___

Longest Tail on a Horse
August 23, 2007

JJS Summer Breeze, or Summer, is a horse. She holds the record for having the world's Longest Tail on a Horse. Her tail is 12 feet 6 inches (381 cm) long! Like Rapunzel's hair in the famous fairy tale, Summer's tail just grew and grew!

Summer belongs to Crystal Socha (USA). Socha washes Summer's tail once every two months. After she washes and dries the tail, Socha braids it. Then, she rolls it up and covers it with a white sock so that Summer can run without dragging her tail on the ground!

● Washing a horse's tail usually does not take long for most horse owners. Summer's case is different though. How long does it take Socha to comb and wash Summer's tail? To find out, complete the puzzle below. Cross out the spaces that contain a number divisible by 3 or 4. Write the remaining letters in order on the lines to spell a message.

10	6	14	24	2	19	12	7	22	4	5
I	A	T	N	T	A	U	K	E	P	S
26	8	9	25	18	32	34	16	38	11	27
A	T	O	B	T	W	O	A	U	T	O
42	26	20	62	35	15	48	58	21	52	49
O	T	R	H	R	Y	S	E	I	X	E
77	36	50	54	56	40	46	60	70	55	S
H	T	O	D	A	Y	U	N	R	S	C

___ ___   ___ ___ ___ ___ ___   ___ ___ ___ ___

___ ___ ___ ___ ___   ___ ___ ___ ___ ___ .

Gee, What a Snail!

Largest Snail
December 1978

Did you know that snails come in many sizes? Some are so small that they can sit on the tip of your finger. Others grow to more than a foot (30 cm) long!

In 1978, Christopher Hudson (UK) owned a giant tiger snail. The snail came from Sierra Leone, a small country in Africa. Hudson's snail was the Largest Snail ever recorded. From snout to tail, it measured 15.5 inches (39.3 cm). The length of its shell was 10.75 inches (27.3 cm). At 2 pounds (900 g), the snail weighed more than two cans of soup! Hudson named his snail Gee Geronimo.

● A snail moves by creeping along slowly. Imagine that you are building a "hill" of small rocks for a snail to climb. If you follow the pattern shown below, how many rocks would you need to build a hill that is 8 rocks high?

_____

How can you solve the problem without drawing all of the rocks?

_____

_____

_____

_____

A Floppy-Eared Lop

Longest Ears on a Rabbit
November 1, 2003

If you have a pet, you are responsible for that pet. You have to feed it, house it, and love it. A rabbit can be a great pet. It is warm and cuddly and can even be house-trained. Taking care of a rabbit is fairly easy. But, if you have an English lop, you have some things to think about—ears! Most rabbits' ears stick up straight, but not lops' ears. Lops have floppy ears that hang down below their chins. An English lop named Nipper's Geronimo holds the record for the Longest Ears on a Rabbit. His ears measure 31.125 inches (79 cm) from one ear tip to the other. His ears are so long and floppy that his owner has to be careful that Nipper doesn't step on them! Because of these enormous ears, Nipper's Geronimo needs a big cage and a lot of room to move around.

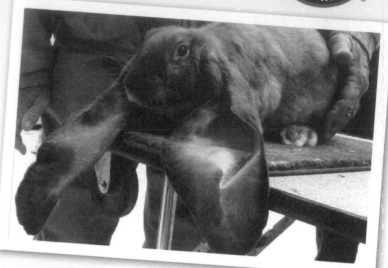

● Below are six named sets of rabbits. The rabbit names are made up of two words that share a common letter. The carrots contain these missing letters. Match the correct carrots to the rabbits by writing the missing letters.

N

ENGLI ____ H
____ POT

L

BELGI ____ N
H ____ RE

R

HOL ____ AND
____ OP

D

SATI ____
A ____ GORA

S

SILVE ____
MA ____ TEN

NETHERLAN ____
____ WARF

A

CD-104534

Here Come the Dogs

Most Dogs Walked Simultaneously by an Individual
September 13, 2008

A person walking a dog isn't an unusual sight. But, what about a person walking 27 dogs at one time? That's what Melissa Crispin Piche (Canada) did! She holds the record for the Most Dogs Walked Simultaneously by an Individual.

Piche owns a dog-walking business, so she knows how to handle dogs. In 2008, she set out on her record-breaking walk. It took place at a park in Alberta, Canada. Piche walked the dogs for 43 minutes, 17 seconds. More than 800 pounds (363 kg) of dog pulled on her as they walked a little more than two miles (3.2 km)!

● **Read the story about Luis and Kate. Using the clues, answer the question. Then, complete the chart to check your guess.**

Luis and Kate each have a dog-walking business. On Day 1, Luis walks 1 dog. On Day 2, he walks 2 dogs. On Day 3, he walks 4 dogs. On Day 4, he walks 7 dogs. The pattern continues for 8 days.

On Day 1, Kate walks 3 dogs. On Day 2, she walks 6 dogs. On Day 3, she walks 9 dogs. On Day 4, she walks 12 dogs. The pattern continues for 8 days.

Who do you think will walk more dogs on Day 7? _____

	Number of Dogs Walked							
	Day 1	Day 2	Day 3	Day 4	Day 5	Day 6	Day 7	Day 8
LUIS	1	2						
KATE	3	6						

Talk About Big-Hearted

Slowest Heart Rate in a Mammal
November 12, 2002

Thump-thump, thump-thump, thump-thump. That's the sound of your heart beating.

Thump-thump, thump-thump!

That's the sound of a blue whale's heartbeat. Because of the blue whales' enormous size, their hearts beat at least 10 times slower than ours. Although blue whales' heart rates range from only 4 to 8 beats per minute, don't worry about missing it. Those huge hearts beat so loud that you can hear them thumping from up to 20 miles (32 km) away!

● The heart is an important body organ. Below are the names of several other body organs. Each name fits onto the sets of lines. The letters from the words BODY ORGANS have been provided for you.

B____ ____ ____ ____

____ ____ O____ ____ ____ ____

____ ____ D____ ____ ____

____ ____ Y____ ____ ____

____ ____ O ____ ____ ____ ____

____ ____ R ____ ____

____ ____ G____

____ A____ ____ ____ ____ ____

____ ____ ____ ____ N ____

____ ____ ____ S ____ ____ ____

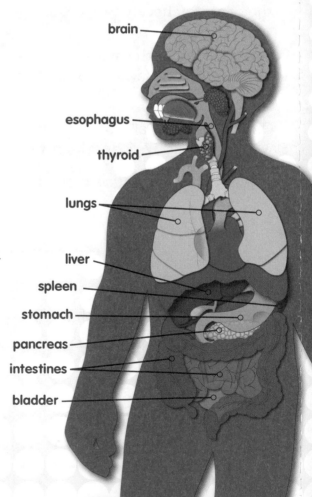

brain
esophagus
thyroid
lungs
liver
spleen
stomach
pancreas
intestines
bladder

CD-104534

Grasshopper Rain

Most Destructive Insect

A desert locust is a type of grasshopper. It is small , measuring 1.8 to 2.4 inches (4.5 to 6 cm) long. It flies alone at night. And, it eats exactly what its body needs. What is so destructive about that? Nothing. When locusts behave this way, they are in what is called the solitarious phase. The locusts are harmless because they are solitary, or all alone. But, if the weather changes, so do the locusts. When more locusts have to fight for the same food, they change their behavior. Instead of flying alone at night, they form daytime swarms numbering in the billions. And, although one locust still eats its body weight in food, a swarm of 50 million can eat the same amount of food in one day that would feed 500 people for a year. This phase is called gregarious. Gregarious locusts are unbelievably destructive. They fly in huge swarms , traveling thousands of miles in search of food. Once locusts swarm, little can be done to stop them.

● Below is a locust swarm cloud buzzing around the puzzle. The puzzle contains the words *solitarious* and *gregarious*. It also contains eight boxed words from the passage. Place the seven words in the correct spaces. The starred letters, in order from top to bottom and left to right, will spell what a swarm of locusts is called.

___ ___ ___ ___ ___

Tiny Wonder

Smallest Living Horse
July 7, 2006

Have you heard of the fairy tale "Thumbelina"? It is about a girl who is no bigger than a thumb. Kay and Paul Goessling (both USA) chose that name for one of their horses. She was born on their farm in 2001. She weighed only 8.5 pounds (3.9 kg) at birth. That's about the size of a newborn human baby!

Now grown, Thumbelina stands about 17.5 inches (44.5 cm) tall. In 2006, she was named the Smallest Living Horse. Today, she helps sick and needy children by letting them come visit her and pet her. It is clear that Thumbelina is a little horse with a very big heart!

● Imagine that the owners of a horse farm are planning to fence off three pieces of land for their horses. The pieces will be shaped like a square, a rectangle, and a triangle. All three will have the same area. The map shows a square piece that has been fenced off. Draw the other two shapes.

Area of a rectangle
length x width

Area of a triangle
½ base x height

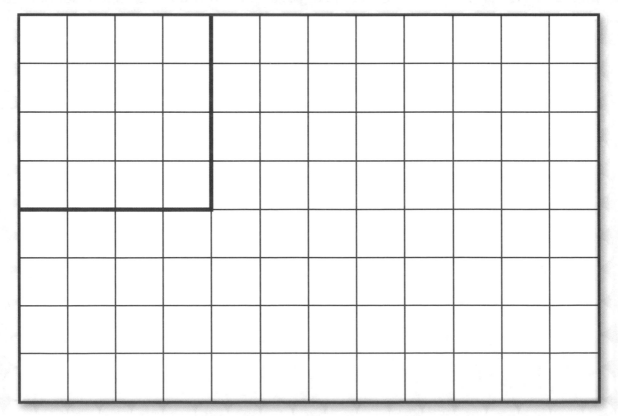

CD-104534

Heavyweight Champ

Largest Species of Beetle

Thousands of different kinds of beetles live throughout the world. They come in different sizes, shapes, and colors. In terms of weight, the Goliath beetle of Africa is the heavyweight champ. In fact, it is the Largest Species of Beetle in the world.

A full-grown Goliath beetle can be as long as 4.5 inches (11.4 cm). Its weight can soar to 3.5 ounces (100 g). That's as much as the weight of 100 paper clips! Put another way, it would take 33,000 ants to equal the weight of this one giant bug!

● Some relatives of the Goliath beetle are pictured on the grid. Each beetle stands for a number. The numbers around the grid are the sums you get when you add the numbers in a row or a column. Figure out the number that each beetle stands for and write the missing sums. Then, write the matching number beside each beetle on the left.

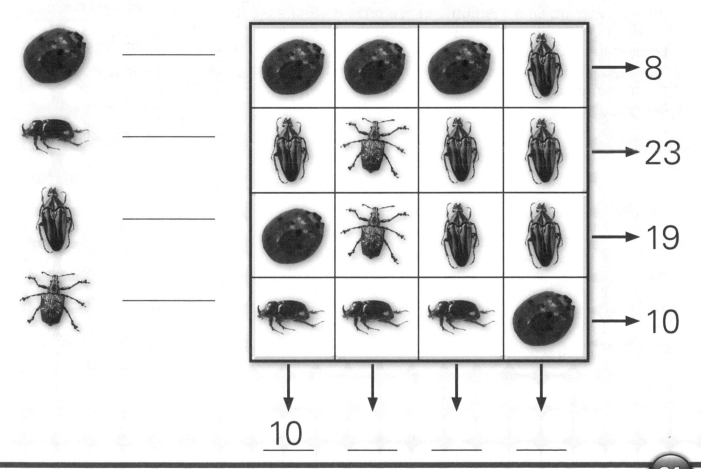

8

23

19

10

10 ___ ___ ___

CD-104534

Dog Power

Heaviest Dog Breed

When you walk your dog on his leash, you want to be able to pull him away from a dangerous situation. But, if your dog happens to be an Old English mastiff or St. Bernard, you might have trouble pulling him anywhere. That's because these breeds share the record for Heaviest Dog Breed in the world. Males regularly grow to a weight of 170 to 200 pounds (77.1 to 90.7 kg). That's heavier than many grown men! The Old English mastiff is taller and thinner than the St. Bernard. But, they're both canine powerhouses.

How much food do you think these dogs eat? Large dogs need at least 20 calories a day for each pound of body weight. That means a 200-pound (90.7-kg) dog needs to eat 4,000 calories a day. That's a lot of calories!

● Kids need about 1,400 to 2,000 calories a day, depending on their weight. One medium cheese pizza contains most of those daily calories, so you can't eat the whole thing! Look at the four pizzas. Each contains a special mix of toppings. For each pizza, unscramble the first letters of the toppings to discover another word to describe these enormous dogs.

anchovies
ham
minced garlic
mozzarella cheese
mushrooms
olives
tomatoes

___ ___ ___ ___ ___ ___ ___

anchovies
extra cheese
ground beef
roast chicken
tomatoes

___ ___ ___ ___ ___

avocado
extra cheese
garlic
lettuce
red peppers

___ ___ ___ ___ ___

avocado
sauce
tomatoes
vegetables

___ ___ ___ ___

Deep-Sea Monster

Earliest Sighting of an Adult Giant Squid
September 30, 2004

Long ago, sailors and fishermen told stories of scary sea monsters. Some of the tales may have been based on the giant squid. This animal grows to be more than 50 feet (15 m) long. It also weighs more than 1,000 pounds (454 kg). With its long, bullet-shaped body and eight arms, it does look a bit like a monster!

In spite of their huge size, adult giant squids are difficult to find. So, very little is known about the animals. In 2004, two Japanese researchers were able to lure one to their ship. It was the first time anyone had ever seen an adult giant squid in its natural habitat. The men excitedly took more than 500 photos. But, four hours after they caught the giant squid, it escaped!

● Learn more facts about the giant squid. Follow the directions on the seaweed in order. Then, write the answers on the lines.

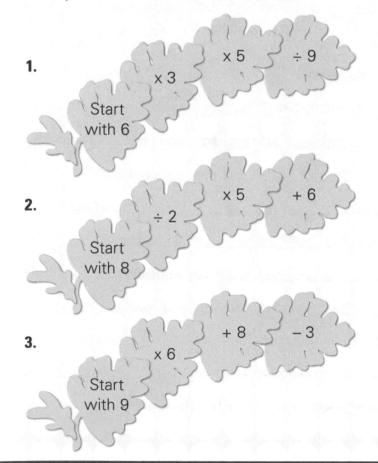

1.
Start with 6 → × 3 → × 5 → ÷ 9

The giant squid has the largest eyes of any animal. Each eye measures _____ inches across.

2.
Start with 8 → ÷ 2 → × 5 → + 6

The giant squid that was photographed in 2004 was _____ feet long.

3.
Start with 9 → × 6 → + 8 → − 3

The largest giant squid measured about _____ feet long.

A Colony of Penguins

Largest Penguin Colony
April 1, 2001

A chinstrap penguin in Antarctica will never get lonely. That's because this flightless bird lives with millions of friends. Zavodovski Island is home to the Largest Penguin Colony in the world. Imagine two million chinstrap penguins waddling around on four million pink webbed feet!

A group of penguins is called a colony. The word *colony* is also used to name a group of termites or bats. What about a colony of reindeer? No, that's called a herd, as in cattle. What about a colony of kangaroos? No, that's called a troop, as in baboons and scouts.

● Below is a list of animal group descriptions with clues. The corresponding animal names are written in the penguin footprints. Using the clues and your knowledge of these animals, try to match each group name with the correct animal.

an ambush of _____ [wild striped cats]

an army of _____ [wet toad cousins]   **jellyfish**   **gorillas**   **wolves**

a band of _____ [jungle apes]

geese   a charm of _____ [tiny birds]   **tigers**

a crash of_____ [huge horned mammals]   **leopards**

frogs   a float of _____ [swimming reptiles]

a gaggle of _____ [noisy honking birds]

lions   a kindle of _____ [cute babies]

toads   a knot of _____ [dry frog cousins]   **giraffes**

hummingbirds   a leap of _____ [quick spotted cats]

a pack of _____ [wild dog cousins]

crocodiles   a pride of _____ [king of the beasts]   **kittens**

a smack of _____ [slimy ocean swimmers]   **rhinoceroses**

a tower of _____ [tall mammals]

CD-104534

Bombing Butterflies

Most Aggressive Butterfly

Imagine a butterfly's wings fluttering against your cheek. Gentle, right? Think again. If you accidentally stumble into a certain butterfly's territory in Uganda, watch out. It may attack. The *Charaxes candiope* has a wingspan that is fairly small, but it is a powerful flier and very protective of its territory. The *Charaxes candiope* is the Most Aggressive Butterfly in the world.

● This butterfly's common name is the Green-Veined Emperor. An emperor is a ruler of a country. But, the Green-Veined Emperor thinks it is a ruler of a territory! Listed below are some butterflies that are named for different types of rulers. Use the scientific names and related clues to figure out the missing words.

	Scientific Name	Clues
1. ___ ___ ___ ___ ___ ___ ___ Leilia	*Asterocampa leilia*	the wife of an emperor
2. ___ ___ ___ ___ ___ butterfly	*Danaus gilippus*	the mother of a princess
3. ___ ___ ___ ___ ___ ___ ___ butterfly	*Danaus plexippus*	a royal ruler
4. ___ ___ ___ ___ ___ ___ Baskettail	*Epitheca princeps*	the brother of a princess
5. ___ ___ ___ ___ s' Skipper	*Euphyes dukesi*	the husband of a duchess
6. ___ ___ ___ ___ 's Hairstreak	*Satyrium kingi*	the father of a princess

What a Crowd!

Largest Colony of Mammals
1901

Did you know that prairie dogs live in groups called towns? These towns are usually made up of hundreds of prairie dogs. The largest known town was discovered in 1901. It was the Largest Colony of Mammals ever found. About 400 million prairie dogs lived there. That number is more than the number of people living in the United States! The town was so large that it stretched from Texas to Mexico!

● **The largest prairie dog town was almost the size of West Virginia. How many square miles did it cover? To find out, read the clues and fill in the boxes on the right. Then, complete the sentence at the bottom of the page.**

• Pick a number that is greater than 20,000 but less than 30,000.

• All of the digits are different.

• The first two digits add up to 5.

• The first three digits add up to 12.

• The last three digits add up to 12.

• The sum of the first two digits equals the last digit.

• The sum of all of the digits is 17.

The largest prairie town covered _____ square miles.

It's Hungry!

Greediest Animal

Babies love to eat. In the first month of life, human babies spend most of their time eating and sleeping. The baby of the polyphemus moth loves to eat too. In fact, this caterpillar has set the world record for being the Greediest Animal. In the first 56 days of its life, it eats an amount that is equal to 86,000 times its weight at birth. That's like a 7-pound (3-kg) human baby eating 273 tons (247.7 t) of food!

● When the caterpillar of the polyphemus moth first hatches, it eats its own eggshell. Later, it feeds on leaves. Learn more facts about this "greedy" animal.
Look at the number patterns below and write the missing numbers. Use the last number in each pattern to complete the sentence.

1.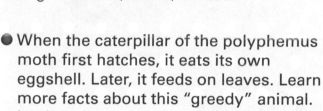
   39 31 24 18

The caterpillar of the polyphemus moth grows to be about _____ inches long.

2. 3½ 3¾ 4 4¼

The adult polyphemus moth has a wingspan of about _____ inches.

3. 3.7 2.9 2.2 1.6

The caterpillar inside the egg is about _____ inches long.

Poisonous Medicine

Most Dangerous Lizard

The Gila monster lives in the deserts of Mexico and the southwestern United States. It is one of only two poisonous lizards in the whole world. It carries enough poison to kill two people! But, because these lizards spend almost all of their time resting in their underground burrows, you shouldn't worry too much.

Gila monsters are large lizards. They can grow to be up to 2 feet (60.96 cm) long and are covered in colorful scales. These lizards are rarely seen because they don't need to hunt very often. When they do, they can eat up to one-third of their body weight at a time. Because the Gila monster doesn't use much energy moving around, one meal will last a long time.

The Gila monster is not all bad news. For people with type-2 diabetes, a disease caused by too much sugar in the blood, the Gila monster's poison is a lifesaving medicine. Scientists have created a diabetic drug from this lizard's fatal venom.

● Below are two lists. The first contains words describing the Gila monster. The second contains opposites of those words. Write the letters on the lines to match the 10 sets of opposites.

Gila Monster Words		Opposites	
1. colorful	____	A. commonly
2. dangerous	____	B. least
3. desert	____	C. medicine
4. grow	____	D. moving
5. large	____	E. northeastern
6. most	____	F. plain
7. poison	____	G. rain forest
8. rarely	____	H. safe
9. resting	____	I. shrink
10. southwestern	____	J. small

A Lazy Life

Longest-Living Animal
October 28, 2007

There's not much excitement when you are an ocean clam. You sit at the bottom of the cold, dark sea, bury yourself in sand, and wait for some tasty algae to float by your shell—day after day, week after week, month after month, and year after year. And, for Ming, a quahog clam found off the coast of Iceland, century after century.

Scientists estimate that Ming was 405 to 410 years old at the time of the clam's discovery. How can scientists tell? They can tell by Ming's growth rings. Like tree trunks, a clam's shell grows larger every year. Although Ming's shell is only about 3.4 inches (8.6 cm) wide, it contains hundreds of rings, some so close together that they are difficult to count.

● Using the dates on Ming's shell, write the dates that you think best match the historical events in the table below.

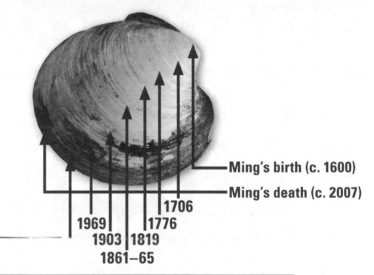

Ming's birth (c. 1600)

Ming's death (c. 2007)

1706
1969 1776
1903 1819
1861–65

Year	Historical Event
	The year of the American Civil War
	The year the American Declaration of Independence was signed
	The year Benjamin Franklin was born
	The year Florida became part of the United States
	The year of the Wright brothers' first successful flight
	The year the first man walked on the moon
	The year you were born

King of the North

Largest Carnivore on Land

There's a reason why the polar bear is sometimes called the "King of the North." This animal is the Largest Carnivore (meat eater) on Land. An adult male measures up to 8 feet 6 inches (2.6 m) long from his nose to his tail. Not only that, but he can also weigh an eye-popping 1,320 pounds (600 kg)! That's more than the combined weights of eight men who weigh 160 pounds (73 kg) each!

In spite of its large size, the polar bear is an excellent swimmer. It has been known to swim more than 62 miles (100 km) across the sea in search of food. When food is scarce, the polar bear can survive for a long time without food. It lives off its thick layer of fat, called blubber. The blubber also protects the polar bear from the cold.

● **Read the clues to help you figure out the weights of three polar bears. (Hint: Find the weights of Cubby and Husky first.)**

Cubby weighs 100 pounds less than Husky.

Husky weighs 100 pounds less than Bruno.

The weights of Cubby and Husky add up to 1,920 pounds.

How much does each polar bear weigh?

Cubby _____ pounds

Husky _____ pounds

Bruno _____ pounds

CD-104534

Remember Me?

Most Tenacious Ant Memory

French biologists have come up with a new twist on the old saying that "elephants never forget." According to their research, ants don't forget either! Scientists raised two species of worker ants together for three months as nest-mates. Then, they separated them for another 18 months. What happened when the ants were reintroduced to each other? Normally ants would fight or flee from the other species. But, these ants didn't. To the scientists' astonishment, the ants from one species were still able to recognize the ants from the other species. The early connection still existed, probably through remembered smell.

● An experiment such as the one above can take many steps to get results. Starting with the phrase ALWAYS REMEMBER, follow the instructions, in order, to obtain your result.

ALWAYS   REMEMBER

_____ _____   **1.** Exchange the position of the words.

_____ _____   **2.** Change WAY to GET.

_____ _____   **3.** Move the last letter of the last word to the first letter of the last word.

_____ _____   **4.** Change all of the A's to O's.

_____ _____   **5.** Remove the second M.

_____ _____   **6.** Exchange the first letter of the first word with the third letter of the second word.

_____ _____   **7.** Change the second consonant to the consonant that follows in the alphabet.

_____ _____   **8.** Delete LE.

_____ _____   **9.** Replace all of the B's with V's.

_____ _____   **10.** Change the first S to F.

Lonesome George

Most Endangered Animal

Lonesome George is the world's Most Endangered Animal. He is the only surviving Pinta Island giant tortoise. Giant tortoises can live up to 200 years. Lonesome George is thought to be between 70 and 80 years old. Unless a mate is miraculously found for George, another of Earth's animals will become extinct.

Lonesome George is a 200-pound (90.7-kg) tortoise. He lives in the Galápagos Islands, 600 miles (965.4 km) west of Ecuador. George spends his time at the Charles Darwin Research Center on the island of Santa Cruz. Scientists have introduced him to female tortoises of related species, but unfortunately, no baby Georges have hatched yet.

● Use the clues to complete the crossword puzzle. (Hint: Read the clues in the order they appear.)

Across

3. The Galápagos Islands are famous for their giant _____.

4. Some of these tortoises are so large that full- _____ people can ride on their backs.

6. Giant tortoises may get into terrible _____ if they flip over onto their backs; the weight of their bodies can crush their lungs.

8. The famous naturalist _____ Darwin rode several giant tortoises.

10. Galápagos comes from the Spanish word for "saddle"; some tortoise _____ are shaped like saddles.

11. Saddle-backed tortoises like _____ George have long necks that they use to reach up to the prickly pear cactus.

14. Smaller Galápagos tortoises have domed shells and shorter _____.

16. Galápagos tortoises compete with each other by stretching up their necks; the tortoise that can _____ the highest is the winner.

17. _____ were approximately 15 species of Galápagos tortoises, but 4 are now extinct.

19. Different types of Galápagos tortoises live on _____ islands in the Galápagos Islands chain.

21. Lonesome George was found in 1971 on Pinta Island, one of the _____ Islands.

Down

1. Lonesome _____ is an herbivore; he eats plants and fruit.

2. One reason these tortoises are on the _____ species list is because of goats.

5. Long ago, when fishermen and sailors sailed _____ to the islands, they brought goats; the goats competed with the tortoises for the same food.

7. A second _____ these tortoises are endangered is that they used to be hunted for their meat.

9. Because he is a type of cold-blooded _____, George spends a lot of his time warming his body in the sun.

12. The female Galápagos tortoise lays her _____ in a hole in the sand.

13. Unlike many _____ kinds of turtles, Galápagos tortoises lay only 2 to 16 eggs at a time; other species of turtles usually lay hundreds of eggs.

15. Galápagos tortoise eggs can be about the shape and _____ of a tennis ball.

18. A warmer nest temperature means the _____ will hatch as females.

20. The Charles Darwin Research Station and the Galápagos National Park work together to prevent the remaining giant tortoises _____ becoming extinct.

Floating Logs?

Largest Crocodilians

What animals quietly sit in the water and are often mistaken for floating logs? If you said "crocodilians," you would be right! This group of animals includes crocodiles and alligators. They have bony coats of armor covering their long bodies. They also have long snouts, short limbs, and thick, powerful tails.

The Largest Crocodilians are saltwater crocodiles. They live in the tropical regions of Asia and the Pacific. Adult males grow to be 14 to 16 feet (4.2 to 4.8 m) long. These large fellows weigh 900 to 1,150 pounds (408 to 520 kg)! That's about half a ton!

● Read the sentences below to learn more facts about the saltwater crocodile. Then, have some number fun! Add two math signs (+, –, x, or ÷) to make the given numbers.

Examples:

Add two signs to make 16.

$$3\ 3\ 7 \longrightarrow 3 \times 3 + 7$$

Add two signs to make 14.

$$2\ 4\ 3\ 6 \longrightarrow 24 \div 3 + 6$$

1. A female saltwater crocodile grows to be about 10 feet long.

Add two signs to make 10. $6\ 3\ 8 \longrightarrow$ _____

2. The largest known saltwater crocodile weighed about 2,200 pounds and measured 23 feet long.

Add two signs to make 23. $5\ 5\ 2 \longrightarrow$ _____

3. A female saltwater crocodile may lay 40 to 62 eggs at one time.

Add two signs to make 40. $8\ 2\ 1\ 0 \longrightarrow$ _____

Add two signs to make 62. $5\ 5\ 5\ 2 \longrightarrow$ _____

CD-104534

A Little Racing Champ

Fastest Ferret
July 11, 1999

People hold dog races and horse races, so why not ferret races? A ferret belongs to the weasel family. On July 11, 1999 a town in North England held a ferret race. Jacqui Adams (UK) entered her pet albino ferret, Warhol. It was the little fellow's first race!

Warhol dashed along a tube 32 feet 10 inches (10 m) long. As he ran, Adams cheered him on. Within seconds, the race was over, and Warhol was named the world's Fastest Ferret. He had finished the course in just under 13 seconds, beating 150 other racers!

● Imagine that the pipes below are used for building racing tubes for ferrets. Which four tubes put together would equal a length of 32 feet 10 inches?

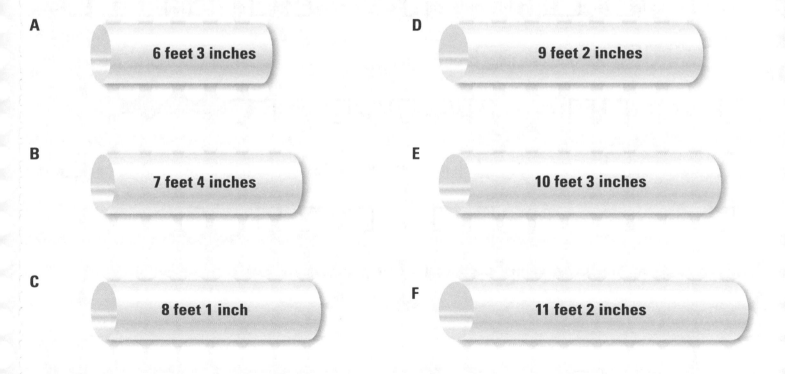

A   6 feet 3 inches

B   7 feet 4 inches

C   8 feet 1 inch

D   9 feet 2 inches

E   10 feet 3 inches

F   11 feet 2 inches

Tubes _____, _____, _____, and _____ have a total length that is equal to the length of Warhol's racing tube.

Living Glass

Most Transparent Amphibians

How can you tell if a frog is alive? When it hops, of course! For many glass frogs of Central and South America, you don't need to wait until they move. You just have to peek through their skin to see if their hearts are beating. Although usually green on top, the bellies of many glass frogs are transparent. You can see right through to their internal organs, including, if you're lucky, their hearts. That's why they are called "glass" frogs. Looking through their bellies is like looking through frosted glasses of water.

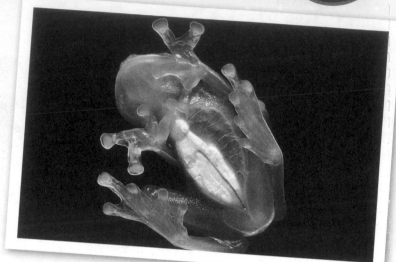

● The sentences below are written as though you are looking at them through a glass of water. Some of the letters are boxed. Read the text and replace the boxed letters with the correct letters. Then, write the letters in order on the lines to spell out a "ribbitty" riddle.

There are no fe☐er t☐☐n 140 differen☐ known spec☐e☐ of gl☐ss ☐☐☐☐s.

Most glas☐☐rogs are less th☐n one inch (2.5 cm) in length. They li☐e high in the treetops

☐f the humid ☐a☐n forests. ☐heir gre☐n bac☐s and t☐☐y size make them

☐ifficult to sp☐t. The female ☐rog lays her eggs on leaves hanging above water. The ☐ale

g☐ards the eggs. When the egg☐ f☐nally hat☐h, t☐e l☐ttle tad☐oles fall into the

water where they remain until t☐ey devel☐☐ into frogs.

_____ ____ __ _____'

_____ _____ ____ _____?

_____-_____!

CD-104534

An Egg-citing Discovery

Largest Dinosaur Eggs
October 1961

In 1961, fossils of dinosaur eggs were found in southeastern France. The eggs were left by a dinosaur named *Hypselosaurus priscus*. This creature lived 80 million years ago. Its eggs are the Largest Dinosaur Eggs discovered so far. With a length of 12 inches (30 cm) long and a diameter of 10 inches (255 mm), they are huge! In fact, they are more than twice the size of ostrich eggs and larger than soccer balls!

● A museum has displayed some dinosaur eggs below. Draw three straight lines to separate the eggs so that each egg is in its own space. (Hint: The spaces do not have to be the same size.)

CD-104534

Police Pal

Smallest Police Dog
November 7, 2006

Midge (USA) works for the sheriff's office in Chardon, Ohio. She doesn't wear a badge or carry a gun though. That's because Midge is a Chihuahua-rat terrier mix. Only 11 inches (28 cm) tall and 23 inches (58 cm) long, Midge holds the record for the world's Smallest Police Dog.

Most police dogs, such as German shepherds, are larger. But, Midge's small size helps her in her job. When she searches buildings, she can get into small spaces easily. Plus, she's not likely to knock over things like larger dogs might. Midge is tiny, but her fellow police officers would probably agree that she is just the perfect size!

● **Learn more facts about Midge. Use the grid to help you write the matching letter for each ordered pair.**

1. Midge's name is short for what name?

___ ___ ___ ___ ___ ___
(2,2) (4,3) (1,4) (6,1) (5,2) (4,5)

2. What does Midge wear when she rides on the sheriff's motorcycle?

___ ___ ___ ___ ___ ___ ___
(6,1) (3,2) (6,1) (6,1) (6,5) (5,2) (3,4)

3. Midge sometimes works with a German shepherd. What is the name of this large dog?

___ ___ ___ ___ ___ ___
(1,1) (2,3) (4,1) (4,5) (4,1) (3,4)

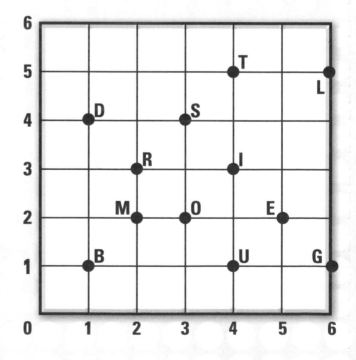

CD-104534

Web Weaving

Strongest Spiderweb

American house spiders are small, about 0.25 inches (6.4 mm) in length. They are shy and are dull colored. They live practically everywhere in the United States. They are not even poisonous. But, these spiders have a special talent: they can build webs so strong that a mouse walking into the sticky silk strands might be lifted right off the ground. Cobweb spiders such as the American house spider spin webs that aren't neat and organized, but they sure are tough!

● Spider silk is incredibly strong and elastic. People use spider silk to make all sorts of things. The puzzle below contains spaces for some of the names of things made from spider silk. The egg sac bubble at the start of each space indicates the word's length. Using the Spider Silk Uses word bank, write the words in the puzzle. Some of the letters have been provided for you.

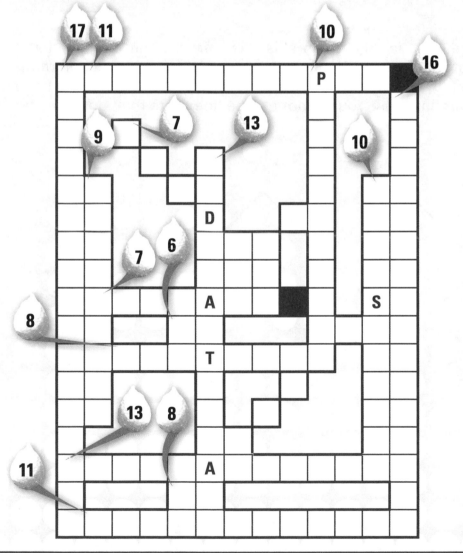

Spider Silk Uses Word Bank

air bags
artificial tendons
bandages
body armor
bridges
bulletproof vests
clothing
fabric
fishing line
medical thread
microscopes
optical fibers
parachutes
telescopes

CD-104534

A Toothy Discovery

Longest Mastodon Tusk
July 28, 2007

Mastodons roamed Earth millions of years ago. They were related to mammoths, and they looked like elephants. In July 2007, a group of scientists found a two-million-year-old tusk in Greece. It measured 16.5 feet (5 m) long. It was the world's Longest Mastodon Tusk.

Along with the tusk, the scientists found parts of the animal's jaws and leg bones. By looking at the findings, the scientists were able to tell that the animal was a male about 25 to 30 years old. He was 11.5 feet (3.5 m) tall. He weighed 6 tons (5.4 t). His weight equaled the weight of three average-sized cars!

● Imagine that you are at a museum to learn about prehistoric animals. The "map" below shows the location of the mastodon display. Begin at Start and follow the direction of the arrows. Trace a path to the display and then return to your starting point. You must trace all of the lines. You may cross over lines, but you cannot trace a line more than once.

Start

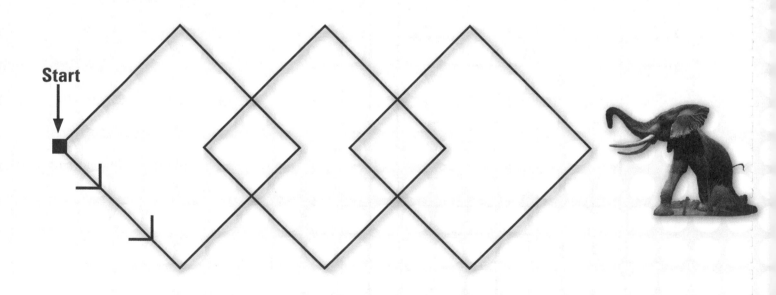

CD-104534

The Mystery of Toyama Bay

Most Bioluminescent Squid

Tourists love to sightsee in Japan's Toyama Bay. They are looking for tiny squid, only 2.4 inches (6 cm) in length. Firefly squid are bioluminescent. They can make their own light. During the day, they remain hidden in deep water. At night, they drift up in search of food. Blue flashing lights on their tentacles attract fish. What makes spring such a wonderful time to see these creatures? It is mating season! To attract a mate, the firefly squid's entire body lights up. The sea glows with lights from millions of swimming firefly squid!

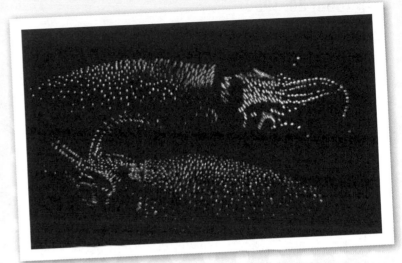

● A squid is a cephalopod. To discover what cephalopod means, fill in the bubbles with the matching words. The bubble groups contain words the same length as the word bank words. Be careful! Some words have the same number of letters, but only one sentence makes sense.

Word Bank				
above	brains	foot	headed	the
because	feet	grow	tentacles	their

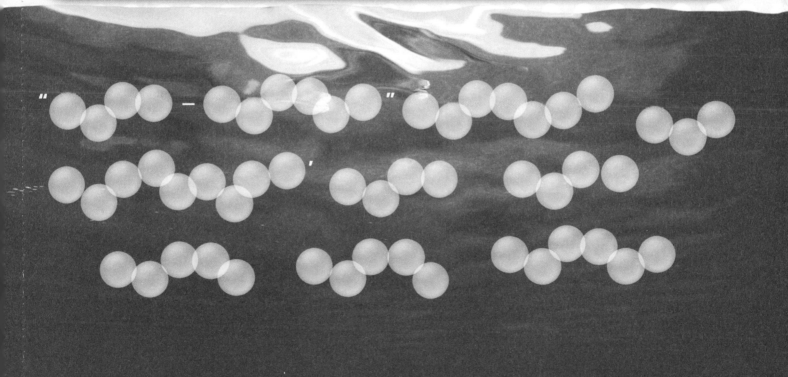

CD-104534

That's One Big Frog!

Largest Frog
October 30, 1989

An African goliath frog hopped into the record books in 1989. It set the record for the Largest Frog in the world. Andy Koffman (USA) found the frog on the Sanaga River in Cameroon in Africa.

Koffman's frog weighed 8 pounds 1 ounce (3.7 kg). That's as much as the weight of a house cat! With its legs stretched out, the frog measured 34.5 inches (87.6 cm). The animal's body took up 14.5 inches (36.8 cm) of the overall length. It was longer than the length of a sheet of notebook paper!

● The goliath frog usually grows to be up to 11.8 inches (30 cm) long. That's about the size of what animal? To find out, read the clues. For each clue, cross out the box with the matching number. Then, rearrange the remaining letters to spell the animal's name.

- It is not ½ of 8.

- It is not ⅓ of 9.

- It is not ⅕ of 10.

- It is not ½ of 14.

- It is not ⅓ of 18.

- It is not ½ of 20.

1 i	4 o	8 b
5 r	10 e	6 n
3 g	11 b	2 d
7 e	9 t	12 a

The African goliath frog is usually about the size of a 6-pound (2.72-kg) pet

___ ___ ___ ___ ___ ___.

Around and Around

Largest Horn Circumference on a Steer
May 6, 2003

Lurch was an African watusi steer (a type of cattle) owned by Janice Wolf (USA). Lurch rose to fame with his supersized horns. They won him the title of the steer with the Largest Horn Circumference. Circumference is the distance around a circle. Lurch's horns measured 37.5 inches (95.25 cm) around!

Two veterinarians examined the horns. They measured his horns three times to be sure of their size. The horns were impressive in other ways too. They had a span of 7 feet (2.1 m). Not only that, but they were also superheavy. Each one weighed more than 100 pounds (45.4 kg)!

● **A circle with a diameter of 12 inches has about the same circumference as one of Lurch's horns. (Hint: The circumference can be found above.)**

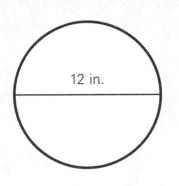

12 in.

Imagine that the circle is placed inside a square.

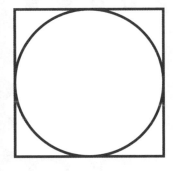

1. Which do you think is greater—the perimeter of the square (the distance around the square) or the circumference of the circle? _____

2. Find the perimeter of the square to check your answer to question 1. _____

3. Which shape has the greater distance around? _____

By how many inches is the distance greater? _____

What a Chatterbox!

Largest Vocabulary for a Living Bird
August 9, 2010

Gabriela "Gaby" Danisch (Germany) has a special pet, Oskar. Oskar loves to talk. He is chattiest in the morning after a good night's sleep. What's so strange about that? Oskar is a small blue bird called a budgerigar. Budgerigars (also called budgies or parakeets) are the most popular pet birds in the world. They are affectionate and smart. Some, like Oskar, can even be trained to talk. Oskar is so clever that he can speak in both Polish and English. With a vocabulary of 148 words and growing, Oskar holds the record for the Largest Vocabulary for a Living Bird. Not only does Oskar say words, but he can also put together short sentences. He loves to dance too!

● Below is list of 15 of Oskar's 148 words. Using the word bank, create five short sentences that Oskar might be able to say.

Word Bank

Australia

come

day

Gaby

good

hello

in

is

my

name

sweet

Tina

to

what's

your

Oskar's Sentences

1. _____

2. _____

3. _____

4. _____

5. _____

6. _____

7. _____

8. _____

9. _____

10. _____

CD-104534

Record-Breaking High Jump

Highest Jump by a Mammal

Can you jump as high as a house? One mountain lion did! It jumped 23 feet (7 m) straight up from the ground and set the record for the Highest Jump by a Mammal. The animal jumped higher than the height of most one-story houses!

A mountain lion may use its jumping skills when hunting. After the animal catches its food, it may hold it in its mouth and leap into a tree before starting its meal.

● Find another name for a mountain lion. Use the ordered pairs to draw points on the grid. Connect the points with a straight line as shown by the arrows. The first three have been done for you. When you are done, a word will appear.

(1,0) ⟶ (1,2) ⟶ (1,4) ⟶ (3,4) ⟶ (3,2) ⟶ (1,2)

(4,4) ⟶ (4,0) ⟶ (6,0) ⟶ (6,4)

(7,0) ⟶ (7,4) ⟶ (8,0) ⟶ (9,4) ⟶ (9,0)

(10,0) ⟶ (10,2) ⟶ (10,4) ⟶ (12,4) ⟶ (12,2) ⟶ (12,0)

(10,2) ⟶ (12,2)

A Super Barker

Loudest Bark by a Dog
June 15, 2009

Daz is a white German shepherd that can really bark! He holds the record for the Loudest Bark by a Dog. His *woof* measured 108 decibels at a special event in London, England. That volume is almost as loud as what you would hear at a live rock concert! Daz's owner, Peter Lucken (UK), says that his dog's bark is amazing. He says that Daz is very lovable and that barking is his way of saying hello!

On the same day that Daz won his record, he took part in a "Dog Chorus." This group of dogs set a record for the Loudest Bark by a Group of Dogs. Their barks measured 115 decibels.

● The old group record was set by 200 dogs in 2008. How many dogs took part in the 2009 Dog Chorus? To find out, divide the box into two matching shapes. The numbers in each shape should add up to the same sum. That sum equals the number of dogs in the chorus. (Hint: The two shapes will not be rectangles.)

5	9	1	10
10	10	10	2
4	6	10	8
1	5	11	2

How many dogs were in the chorus? _____

Giddyup! Up! Up!

Tallest Horse Living
January 19, 2010

● Read the following paragraph and write the missing letters. Then, write the boxed letters in order on the lines at the bottom of the page to discover the names of three of the largest breeds of horses living today.

[ ]ony ride anyone? If it's the USA's Big Jake you want to mount, you'll ne[ ]d a ladder! Big Jake isn't a pony. He's the world's Tallest Ho[ ]se Living. From the bottom of his hooves to the top of his shoulders, he measures almost 6 feet 11 inches (210.8 cm) tall. His [ ]olossal head rises even hig[ ]er. In the horse world, hors[ ]s are measured in "hands," not feet. One hand equals 4 inches (10.2 cm). Although Big Jake has hooves instead of finge[ ]s, he is still 20 hands 2.75 inches (82.75 inches, 210.19 cm) tall. And, that's with[ ]ut his big steel shoes.

Big Jake is a Belgian draft horse. Draft horses like Belgia[ ]s are very large. Big Jake work[ ] as a "hitch horse." He is hit[ ]hed to a wagon that he pul[ ]s with a team of other horses. Jake and his team perform at fairs in Wisconsin and nearb[ ] states.

At birth, Big Jake alrea[ ]y weighed 240 pounds (109 kg), more than most grown m[ ]n. Now, he weigh[ ] more than a ton. He is even taller than some Asian elephants. His appetite matches his huge size. He eats about 40 pounds (18.14 kg) of hay an[ ] 8 gallons (35.24 L) of oats every d[ ]y. That's the same as you eating 256 bow[ ]s of cereal and 54 box[ ]s of cracker[ ] every day!

Belgians, ___ ___ ___ ___ ___ ___ ___ ___ ___ ___ ___ ___, and

___ ___ ___ ___ ___ ___ ___ ___ ___ ___ ___ ___ ___ are

three of the largest breeds of horses alive today.

How Shocking!

Most Electric Fish

Did you know that some fish give off electric charges that can shock you? The electric eel is probably the best known of them all. This snake-like fish lives in the rivers of northern South America. It grows to be about 6 feet (1.8 m) long and weighs 44 pounds (20 kg).

The electric eel holds the record for the Most Electric Fish. Its charge can measure up to 650 volts. That's five times the power of a wall socket in your home! The shock from an electric eel can stun an adult person, and its charge is strong enough to turn on a lightbulb!

● To produce electricity, electric charges flow along a path called a circuit. Complete the math "circuit" below by following the numbered steps. Write the result of each step on the lines on the left. If you follow the steps correctly, you will always be led to the number 1,089. (Try this activity twice and see for yourself!)

First Try

1. _____

2. _____

3. _____

4. _____

5. _____

Second Try

1. _____

2. _____

3. _____

4. _____

5. _____

1,089

1. Choose a three-digit number. The first digit must be at least 2 greater than the last digit.

5. Add the answers from steps 3 and 4.

2. Reverse the order of the digits. (Example: 941 becomes 149)

4. Reverse the order of the digits in the answer to step 3.

3. Subtract the number in step 2 from the number in step 1.

A Spiral Mystery

Most Mysterious New Animal
1994

The Most Mysterious New Animal in the world is, well, mysterious. Rumors of the existence of a *Pseudonovibos Spiralis* in Vietnam and Cambodia have been around for centuries. Scientists are still not sure if this animal exists. In fact, the name means "Fake New Cattle with Spiral Horns." Locally, the people call the mammal the Holy Goat, the Snake-Eating Cow, the Liana-Horned Gaur, and the Spiral-Horned Ox. With no photographs of the mysterious creature, the only evidence of its existence is the discovery of strangely spiraled horns.

● **Using the word bank, write the missing words in the paragraph.**

Word Bank

Cambodia	leopards	rivers	sugarcane	Vietnam
cow	mosquitoes	Sea	tropical	vultures
flooding	pythons	snakebites	typhoons	yak
horns	rice	soybeans	unpredictable	

The ___ ___ ___ ___ ___ of the *Pseudonovibos Spiralis* are said to cure

___ ___ ___ ___ ___ ___ ___ ___ ___ ___. This animal is related to the ___ ___ ___,

gaur, and ___ ___ ___. They live in southeastern ___ ___ ___ ___ ___ ___ ___ and inland

___ ___ ___ ___ ___ ___ ___ ___, close to the South China ___ ___ ___. The land is

very hilly with many ___ ___ ___ ___ ___ ___ and streams. Local crops are the cassava

root, ___ ___ ___ ___, corn, ___ ___ ___ ___ ___ ___ ___ ___ ___, tree nuts, and

___ ___ ___ ___ ___ ___ ___ ___. The climate is ___ ___ ___ ___ ___ ___ ___ ___, and

the weather is ___ ___ ___ ___ ___ ___ ___ ___ ___ ___ ___ ___ ___ with occasional

___ ___ ___ ___ ___ ___ ___ ___ and frequent ___ ___ ___ ___ ___ ___ ___ ___.

The *Pseudonovibos Spiralis* shares the land with many other animals, including elephants,

___ ___ ___ ___ ___ ___ ___ ___, gibbons, ___ ___ ___ ___ ___ ___ ___ ___,

rhinoceroses, ___ ___ ___ ___ ___ ___ ___ ___ and lots and lots of

___ ___ ___ ___ ___ ___ ___ ___ ___ ___.

What a Catch!

Most Tennis Balls Held in the Mouth by a Dog
July 6, 2003

Most kids like to play catch. Most dogs do too, and they are usually pretty good at it. But, golden retriever Augie (USA) is more than just pretty good. He is absolutely amazing. Not only does Augie fetch tennis balls thrown for him, but he also trots back with all of the balls in his mouth. In 2003, he returned with all five balls in his mouth at the same time! Augie's jaws aren't any larger than those of other dogs his size. He's just a brilliant retriever.

Golden retrievers were bred for fetching, or retrieving, things without biting them. They are named for both their beautiful golden color and for their ability to retrieve. Many dog breeds were originally named for what they did (fetch, guard, or herd). Others were named for a place, their appearance, a breeder, or even for artists who liked painting their pictures. Hybrids are a cross between two or more breeds and often have unusual names such as Puggle.

● The word search below contains 35 dog breed names. Words may be found horizontally, vertically, and diagonally. All 35 names are listed in the word bank and are organized by the reason for which they were named. Draw a line through each word in the puzzle as you find it.

WORD BANK — MULTIPLE REASONS
GOLDEN RETRIEVER (color/retrieves things)
INCA HAIRLESS (Peru/hairless)
SAPSALI (Korea/chases away evil)

WORD BANK — HYBRIDS
BOWZER (basset hound and mini schnauzer)
BRAT (rat terrier and Boston terrier)
BUGGS (Boston terrier and pug)
JATZU (Japanese chin and shih tzu)
MALTIPOO (Maltese and poodle)

WORD BANK — PURPOSE
BORZOI (Russian for "swift")
BULLDOG (controls bulls)
OTTERHOUND (finds otters)
POINTER (points to birds)
SETTER (sets animals by crouching)
SHEEPDOG (guards sheep)
SPRINGER SPANIEL (causes animals to spring)
TAIGAN (hunts by speed and sight)
TERRIER (finds rodents)
WHIPPET (moves quickly)

```
S  H  E  E  P  D  O  G  W  S  A  P  S  A  L  I
E  A  V  S  A  M  O  Y  E  D  Y  B  T  W  S  N
T  O  S  A  P  C  O  B  A  A  T  R  A  H  A  C
T  E  R  R  I  E  R  E  E  R  D  A  I  I  I  A
E  T  B  U  L  L  D  O  G  R  M  T  G  P  N  H
R  O  M  A  L  T  I  P  O  O  M  A  A  P  T  A
B  Y  T  R  O  G  R  E  A  T  D  A  N  E  B  I
U  P  E  T  N  T  R  I  B  P  O  I  N  T  E  R
G  O  L  D  E  N  R  E  T  R  I  E  V  E  R  L
G  O  A  B  A  R  B  E  T  T  I  E  J  V  N  E
S  D  N  K  K  E  H  B  T  R  A  T  A  B  A  S
P  L  D  C  I  N  B  O  R  Z  O  I  T  E  R  S
I  E  S  O  S  T  L  W  U  D  T  W  Z  A  D  E
T  E  E  R  H  P  A  Z  D  N  W  A  U  G  N  T
Z  E  E  G  U  R  S  E  P  A  D  N  I  L  E  Y
S  P  R  I  N  G  E  R  S  P  A  N  I  E  L  L
```

WORD BANK — PLACES
AKITA (Japan)
ARMANT (Egypt)
BRITTANY (France)
KISHU (Japan)
TOSA (Japanese city)

WORD BANK — PEOPLE
DOBERMAN (breeder)
LANDSEER (painter)
PLOTT (breeder)
SAINT BERNARD (monk)
SAMOYED (tribe)

WORD BANK — APPEARANCE
BARBET ("beard")
BEAGLE ("small")
CORGI ("dwarf dog")
GREAT DANE (huge)
PAPILLON ("butterfly"; for fringed ears)
SPITZ ("pointed face")
TOY POODLE (tiny)

The unused letters, in order from top to bottom and left to right, will spell the names of two main dog breeds that were bred together to produce the golden retriever.

___ ___ ___ ___-___ ___ ___ ___ ___ ___   ___ ___ ___ ___ ___ ___ ___ ___ ___

___ ___ ___ ___   ___ ___ ___ ___ ___

___ ___ ___ ___ ___   ___ ___ ___ ___ ___ ___

CD-104534

Tiny but Mighty

Most Dangerous Ant

If you visit Australia, make sure you stay away from the bulldog ant. This insect is less than an inch (2.5 cm) long, but as its name suggests, it is fierce! In fact, this tiny creature is considered the Most Dangerous Ant in the world. It uses its powerful sting and strong jaws when it attacks.

The bulldog ant is tiny, but it shows little fear of much bigger animals. In fact, it is not even afraid of people. Anyone who sees the nest of a bulldog ant should stay away. It can spot intruders from 6 feet (1.8 m) away and may give chase!

● The ants below are sitting in a square box. Draw two more squares to separate the ants so that each ant is in its own space. (Hint: The squares will not be the same size.)

CD-104534

"Eye" See You!

Largest Eye-to-Body Ratio

The vampire squid looks as if it came out of a science fiction movie! It has a body that looks like jelly. It also has eight long arms that are webbed. On top of that, the animal has extremely large eyes for its size.

The vampire squid has the Largest Eye-to-Body Ratio of any animal. Its body is up to 11 inches (28 cm) long, while each eye measures 0.9 inches (2.5 cm) across. That would be like a 5-foot (152-cm) person having eyes that measure almost 6 inches (15 cm) across! The vampire squid's eyes are large because the animal lives deep in the ocean where it is dark. The large eyes are able to gather as much light as possible in the dim surroundings.

● A vampire squid's eyes are as big as the eyes of what full-grown animal? To find out, color the circles that contain a number greater than 0.5. When you are done, a word will appear. Write the word on the line.

_____

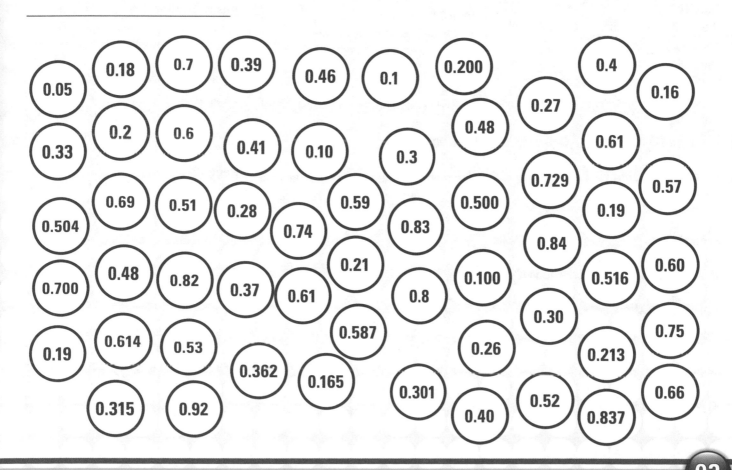

Answer Key

Page 6
carpets; clothes; egg cartons; furniture; lawn chairs; pipes; tile; traffic lights

Page 7
attack; bigger; all; calf; mothers; breathes; weighs; heads; mammals; calves; have; killer whale

Page 8
13

Page 9
Rana; rang; ring; ding; dine; line; life

Page 10
Answers will vary.

Page 11
1. 15; 2. 20; 3. 15; 4. 30

Page 12

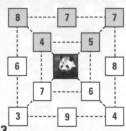

Page 13
1. slug; 2. fish; 3. bug; 4. wolf; 5. fly; 6. chicken; 7. monkey; 8. duck

Page 14
The jump rope costs $1.25, and the ball costs $0.50.

Page 15
tunnel; limbo; owner's; soccer; bottom; basketball; uprights; dance; Einstein

Page 16

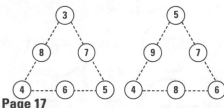

Page 17
crustaceans; fish oil; fish eggs; flying fish; herring; krill; plankton; squid; good luck

Page 18
1. closed; 2. 16, 20

Page 19
banana

Page 20
20 squares (13 small squares, 6 medium squares, 1 large square)

Page 21
1. naked mole rat; 2. fangtooth; 3. crocodile; 4. walrus; 5. great white shark; 6. sheep

Page 22
Pekingese; emperor; record; dogs; sleeves; straight; tongue

Page 23
256

Page 24
Answers will vary; B is the same distance from A as it is from C.

Page 25
sea dragon

Page 26
9 jumps (On the first jump, the frog is up 5 feet. On the second jump, the frog is up another 5 feet or 10 feet total. On the third jump, the frog is up 15 feet. By the eighth jump, the frog is up 40 feet to the top of the pit. On the ninth jump, the frog leaps 10 feet and is out of the pit.)

Page 27
1. 635 + 47 = 682; 537 - 14 = 523
2. 263 + 189 = 452; 719 - 243 = 476
3. 704 + 228 = 932; 951 - 587 = 364

Page 28
1. insects, 2. scorpions, 3. honey, 4. pollen, 5. seeds, 6. nectar, 7. fruit, 8. worms, 9. spiders, 10. nuts

Page 29
You will need three 5-inch blocks and four 7-inch blocks.

Page 30
Puma names are brown tiger; cabcoh; gato monte; catamount; cougar; deer cat; ghost cat; king cat; leopardo; mountain lion; night screamer; painter; panther; reditigri. Non-puma names are Andean mountain cat; bobcat; caucel; chinchay; gatillo; jaguar; kodkod; lince; lynx; margay; ocelot; oncilla; otter cat; pampas cat; pumilla; tigrillo

Page 31
26

Page 32
buzzworm

Page 33
Thumper, Wiggles, Cotton, Fluffy

Page 34

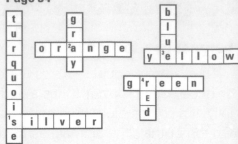

Smasher

Page 35
Answers will vary but may include bossy bird; cheery chicken; curious cat; fast fish; gentle gerbil; goofy guinea pig; hungry horse; lazy lizard; messy mouse; rascally raccoon; slithery snake; trusting turtle

Page 36
1. 60; 2. 96

Page 37
12th day of the month

Page 38
1. H; 2. A; 3. G; 4. C; 5. I; 6. F; 7. J; 8. E; 9. B; 10. D

Page 39
13, 6, 11; 8, 10, 12; 9, 14, 7

Page 40
Answers will vary but may include S–scorpion (smaller); W–wildebeest (taller); A–alligator (smaller); L–lion (about the same); L–llama (taller); O–owl (smaller); W–wolf (about the same)

Page 41
Elephants; with; smaller; strangely; nose; people; mostly; eastern; shaped; Mammal; or; light; record; star-nosed mole

Page 42

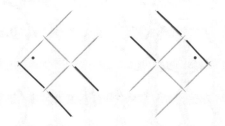

Page 43
give people rides; play the harmonica; gather sticks; haul logs; give massages; play darts; play with a soccer ball; dance; *goon chaawn*

CD-104534

Answer Key

Page 44

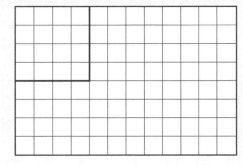

```
          183
        90   93
      40   50   43
    13   27   23   20
  4    9   18    5   15

          110
        50   60
      30   20   40
    21   9   11   29
  15   6    3    8   21
```

Page 45

1. D; 2. A; 3. F; 4. H; 5. I; 6. E; 7. B; 8. G; 9. C; 10. J

Page 46

7, 5

Page 47

master of the grasses

Page 48

some; sharks; heating; that; heat; but; must; keeping; brains; hot; hunting

Page 49

14

Page 50

Answers may vary, but examples are 1. cow K walk; 2. frog E jump; 3. hamster C dig; 4. kangaroo F leap; 5. lizard B crawl; 6. monkey A climb; 7. rabbit D hop; 8. sea gull H soar; 9. fox G run; 10. swordfish I swim; 11. worm L wiggle; 12. zebra J trot

Page 51

Tupper–black, 36 inches; Chip–brown, 27 inches; Lacy–white, 18 inches

Page 52

be; bet; tube; brute; butter; I; it; eat; tail; butterfly tail

Page 53

bite; is; owner; poisonous; and; Rosi

Page 54

It takes about three hours.

Page 55

36 rocks (Find the pattern: 1 + 2 + 3 + 4 + 5 + 6 + 7 + 8.)

Page 56

English spot; Holland lop; silver marten; Belgian hare; satin angora; Netherland dwarf

Page 57

Luis; Chart should read: Luis 1, 2, 4, 7, 11, 16, 22, 29; Kate 3, 6, 9, 12, 15, 18, 21, 24.

Page 58

Brain; stOmach; blaDder; thYroid; esOphagus; liveR; lunGs; pAncreas; spleeN; inteStines

Page 59

PLAGUE, small; type; once; swarms; phase; eats; flying; huge

Page 60

The rectangle and the triangle should be drawn to show that each one has an area of 16 square units. Here is one configuration:

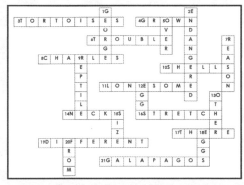

Page 61

ladybug, 1; black beetle, 3; green beetle, 5; striped beetle, 8; The missing sums are 20, 14, and 16.

Page 62

mammoth; great; large; vast

Page 63

1. 10; 2. 26; 3. 59

Page 64

tigers; frogs; gorillas; hummingbirds; rhinoceroses; crocodiles; geese; kittens; toads; leopards; wolves; lions; jellyfish; giraffes

Page 65

Empress Leilia; Queen butterfly; monarch butterfly; Prince Baskettail; Dukes' Skipper; King's Hairstreak

Page 66

23,705

Page 67

1. 39, 31, 24, 18, 13, 9, 6, 4, 3; 3 inches; 2. 3½, 3¾, 4, 4¼, 4½, 4¾, 5, 5¼, 5½; 5½ inches, 3. 3.7, 2.9, 2.2, 1.6, 1.1, 0.7, 0.4, 0.2, 0.1; 0.1 inches

Page 68

1. F; 2. H; 3. G; 4. I; 5. J; 6. B; 7. C; 8. A; 9. D; 10. E

Page 69

1706, The Year Benjamin Franklin was born; 1776, The year the American Declaration of Independence was signed; 1819, The year Florida became part of the United States; 1861–65, The year of the American Civil War; 1903, The Year of the Wright brothers' first successful flight; 1969, The year the first man walked on the moon; _ _ _ _, The year you were born

Page 70

Cubby, 910 pounds; Husky, 1,010 pounds; Bruno, 1,110 pounds

Page 71

always remember; 1. remember always; 2. remember algets; 3. remember salget; 4. remember solget; 5. remeber solget; 6. lemeber sorget; 7. leneber sorget; 8. neber sorget; 9. never sorget; 10. never forget

Pages 72–73

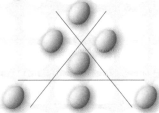

Page 74

1. 6 x 3 – 8; 2. 5 x 5 – 2; 3. 8 ÷ 2 x 10, 55 + 5 + 2

Page 75

A, B, C, F

Page 76

What is a frog's favorite kind of music? Hip-hop!

Page 77

Page 78

1. Midget; 2. goggles; 3. Brutus

CD-104534

Answer Key

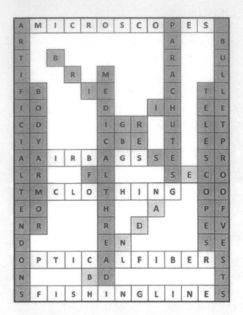

Page 80

Flip design for alternate answer.

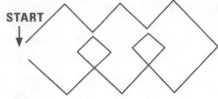

Page 81

"foot-headed" because the tentacles' feet grow above their brains

Page 82

rabbit

Page 83

1. Answers will vary; 2. 48 inches (Each side of the square is 12 inches.);
3. square; 10.5 inches

Page 84

Answers will vary. Some of Oskar's real sentences: Good day. What's your name? Tina is in Australia. Hello my sweet. Come to Gaby.

Page 85

puma

Page 86

52

Page 87

Percherons, Clydesdales

Page 88

Answers will vary.

Page 89

horns; snakebites; cow; yak; Vietnam; Cambodia; Sea; rivers; rice; sugarcane; soybeans; tropical; unpredictable; typhoons; flooding; pythons; vultures; leopards; mosquitoes

Pages 90–91

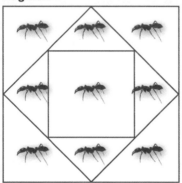

wavy-coated retriever and tweed water spaniel

Page 92

Page 93

dog